**Private Lives
and
Public Accounts**

For Mr. and Mrs. Sylvan Tobin:
Thank you so very much
for being an MSPP Friend.
Your support is deeply
appreciated.

Warmly,
Tim

Private Lives and Public Accounts

Thomas J. Cottle

University of Massachusetts Press
Amherst, 1977

Copyright © 1977 by Thomas J. Cottle
All rights reserved
Library of Congress Catalog Card Number 77-73476
ISBN 0-87023-240-1
Printed in the United States of America
Designed by Mary Mendell
Library of Congress Cataloging in Publication Data
appear on the last printed page of the book.

For
Eloise Frazier Mikkelsen
and
Edwin C. Mikkelsen

Let me thank first the Massachusetts Institute of Technology, and in particular Dr. Merton Kahne and Dr. Benson R. Snyder. Also, The Children's Defense Fund of the Washington Research Project, Marian Wright Edleman, Director; The Guggenheim Foundation; and The Field Foundation, and in particular, Leslie Dunbar.

Special thank you's must go as well to Nelson Aldrich, Max Birnbaum, Malcolm Call, James Cass, Diane Divoky, Alec Fleming, David Gottlieb, Anne Hird, Oliver W. Holmes, Paul Houts, Dennis Jaffe, Michael I. Kessler, Jennifer King, Gene Lichtenstein, Sara Lawrence and Orlando B. Lightfoot, Sally Makacynas, Gary T. Marx, Cynthia Merman, Anne and Martin Peretz, Gerald M. Platt, Joseph Pleck, Peter Raggatt, Viviette Reynell, Lillian Rubin, Carol Schoen, Peter Schrag, James Small, Cynthia Sparrow, Arthur Shostak, Jerry Williamson, and always, Kay Cottle.

Finally, I want to thank all of the people whose words appear in this book. Always, their contribution is enormous.

Acknowledgments

Contents

This book is about people, the lives they lead, the situations they create and in which they find themselves, and especially the ways in which they speak about their lives and these situations. It is based on a series of conversations and observations which fall in the tradition of what social scientists call naturalistic or participant observation. That is, the conversations did not grow out of any predetermined set of questions or plan of inquiry, but rather out of months and years of friendships and associations. The point of these conversations was to allow people to speak freely about themselves and the circumstances of their lives, so that one might derive a sense not only of how these people lead their lives, but also of how they recount their lives, define their private and public situations, and account for their personal and shared experiences.

The purpose in writing this book was not to present people and their experiences in an objective and dispassionate manner. Instead, this book is of a subjective nature, a personal enterprise in which the researcher made no attempt to hide his involvement in the conversations and situations portrayed, or deny the degree to which he became implicated in the life histories under study. Thus, if this book does not belong to the tradition of humanistic sociology, psychiatry, and anthropology, it is at least an attempt to contribute to these traditions.

As the title suggests, this book is concerned with the matter of observing human behavior as well as with observing ourselves as we make our observations. It is also concerned with relationships between ourselves and those with whom we converse, on the one hand, and between the social, cultural, or so-called publicly shared features of human existence and the more intimate features of the private life, on the other. These relationships—which are discussed more fully in the first two chapters—are complicated by the fact that conversation, no matter how personal its substance, is a public experience. In effect then, when we say we are interested in the expression of private lives, we are making a somewhat paradoxical statement. For in the simplest terms, what we hear and observe of another person or an event in which we are even minimally involved, necessarily is influenced by *our* presence. This is precisely one of the issues we will take up in later chapters.

One thing more about the so-called public aspect of personal recounting. All social situations, whether they flow naturally in the course of one's life or are created through a method of social scientific inquiry of the type we will be examining, are constituted in part by political realities, both historical and contemporary. While this point will be stressed explicitly and implicitly throughout the book, it must be said at the outset that no form of social inquiry, even one making claims to humanistic traditions and ethics, can escape these political influences. Merely to live is to make a political statement of one sort or another, for to live is to respond to the political and economic realities that shape one's public and private worlds.

The book is divided into four sections. Section One examines the method of inquiry employed, some personal reasons and justifications for its use, and more generally, the problems of personal divulgence and privacy. Sections Two and Three focus on observations of the lives of children and adults, some poor, some affluent, some faring better than others. Section Four turns our attention to observations of public situations in which group or social behavior assumes greater importance than the concentration on a single life. Finally, the Epilogue serves as a reminder not only of the sensitivity of all of our personal and social observations, but also of the political context in which our lives unfold, and the political messages, witting and unwitting, that emerge from our social scientific inquiries.

This discussion of private lives and public accounts begins with my conversation with a man who evokes some of the elements of the method of inquiry and conceptual concerns dealt with in this book. One of the principles of my work is to allow people to speak for themselves, to whatever extent this is possible, and in return to communicate to them, in our conversations as well as in my writing, that it is their words I seek, and not material for the generation of something that ultimately transcends their words, and hence their lives. Accordingly, it is only appropriate that this work commence with a fragment of a conversation in which both participants, in their respective manners, attend to one another's private lives and public accounts.

Part One

On Making Personal Observations

One has to know Paulo Marcucci to know the way he speaks. One can recapture his words, even transcribe them accurately enough, and still not sense the richness of his language, his presentation in conversation. Paulo himself claims there is nothing special about the way he talks, but he knows he has a wondrous quality in his speech, an aliveness that is often so theatrical, people sitting with him spontaneously break into applause. "Man's fantastic, isn't he?" they'll mutter aloud. "You should be on television, Paulo. How many times you been told that?"

"I used to dance on television," Paulo Marcucci will respond.

"Oh yeah?" The men in the cafeteria are more than a little impressed, but distrustful at the same time.

"Yeah, it's true," Paulo Marcucci shouts at them, with the same serious face he wears coming out of church every morning. "I danced on the television until my father told me to get the hell off before I broke it."

The men laugh and applaud and whistle. Paulo Marcucci is delighted with himself. He is the hit of the moment.

Sitting next to him drinking a capucino that in this one Boston cafeteria is so sweet Gino has warned me it will rot my tongue along with my teeth, I said to my friend of several years: "And you say you speak just like all the rest of us. You're the poor man's Milton Berle."

He put one of his hands on my hand and gestured as if he were about to clamp his other hand over my mouth. "Please," he whispered loudly enough so that his audience could hear. "Tony Bennett. Antonio Benedetto, huh? Not Milton Berle. And where do you come off calling me a poor man?"

"I didn't mean that you were poor," I responded sheepishly, realizing how my remark could have been misinterpreted.

"What, you think *they're* poor?" Paulo gestured toward the men who, amused, were watching and listening to our conversation, and waiting for Paulo to nail me to the wall.

"No. I didn't mean. All I meant . . ."

"Please," he said with a smile starting to form. "We're working class, with an emphasis on the class, not poor. We're not poor because we don't pass the Marcucci Poor Man's Test."

Now it was I who sat straight-faced, determined not to ask about the Marcucci Poor Man's Test.

"You don't want to know?" he blurted out, seeing his straight man had quit.

"Go ahead," I mumbled.

"Poor man don't eat, poor man don't laugh."

"That true?"

"How do I know what I'm saying? Am I a psychologist? I make things up. I keep my eyes open and I make things up about people, things that make me feel good about myself. If they're true, they're true; if they aren't, what do I care? I still feel better about myself."

As the conversation appeared to be growing serious, the others began losing interest in what Paulo had to say, and I had all to myself this gentleman of fifty-five, a father of three children, a man who has fought the battle of unemployment for more than ten years.

"How long have I known you?" he asked, with a peculiar sternness in his voice.

"Five years. More than that." My answer sounded like a school boy's response to his teacher.

"Five years and I still don't see what the hell you get out of talking with people like us. Who gives a damn about us? Who do you know, honest to God now, you have one friend in the world who wants to know about people like me, people who haven't done a damn thing in their lives that would make news? You know what Italians are supposed to be? We're singers or we're Mafioso. Right? So who wants to hear about Paulo Marcucci or any of the other guys here, some of which don't even speak English. Even if you wrote in Italian, nobody around here would give you nickel to hear about them. So who cares? You make a few friends, but what does it lead to? What's the point?

"Look, if you got a man, like he's working in an office on Tremont Street, okay? He's got a wife and a couple of kids. He gets good money for what he does. Guy has a nice home out in the suburbs somewhere. What's he want to know about Marcucci and his cafeteria drop-outs for? He couldn't give you a reason in the world. You write books, right? He doesn't want your books. You know what he wants? He wants Mario Puzo. You know Mario Puzo?"

"Not personally."

"You know who I mean though. He wants action, mystery, love, killing, gansters. You take and level this whole part of the city, push the people into the ocean, you thinks he gives a damn! He couldn't care less what you do to us. Give us jobs, take jobs away from us. He doesn't care. He eats, we eat. He laughs, we laugh. Doesn't phase him in the slightest. I've told you things so private and personal, gossip, you could write it out for him and draw pictures on top and photographs on top of that, and he wouldn't look twice at it. Not twice. I'll tell you something. If I was him, if I had that nice steady job with the big home in the suburbs and the two-car garage and everything else that goes with that life, I wouldn't look twice at that stuff myself. Even if it was *me* you were writing about. Maybe I'd look once before I die, like I look at some of the old photographs we got once in a while, but if I never saw them again, what the hell, I'd say. What the hell."

"You wouldn't miss it," I said in a flat tone.

"I wouldn't miss nothing. I'm interested in my life 'cause its *my* life. Somebody else's life living like me, what do I need it for? You want another capucino? Maybe it could rot out your whole mouth."

"I'll take the capucino and I'll tell you something, Tony Bennett. I don't believe you. You have a great sensitivity about what you see and hear. Your life matters plenty, and so do the lives of these people in here. You're furious with that guy in his office for not being interested in you, the same way I am. Nobody likes people not taking interest in us. You're right that outrageous types get in the news, but your life isn't a bunch of old photographs. Not in the least, and you damn well know it isn't. What about that time you and I went through the photographs in that Havana cigar box and you gave me a lecture on each one? That Uncle Guilliamo of yours? You wouldn't care if you never saw a picture of him again?"

"You remember Guilliamo?"

"I don't remember half of what you remember. You do a great act, Marcucci, but I still take everything you say with a grain of you-know-what. The crime is that no one does pay attention to human problems unless they're experiencing them themselves. Guys like you, other families I see, everybody has a way of not having to look at them or hear about them. You know as well as I do that the guy you want to have listen to you is that guy in the office. The government could care less, so it's that guy you want to educate."

"What do you mean educate?" Now Paulo was the school boy, I the teacher.

"You know exactly what I mean. Private things you keep for yourself. The conditions of your life that are caused by society, by all the life styles and laws and policies and institutions all the rest of us practice and uphold. Those conditions are what you want the world to know about. All right, my sermon's over. Now my mouth can rot with your lousy capucino."

Paulo Marcucci was sitting up straight in his chair. His deep brown eyes were flashing as though he wanted to tell me ten million things simultaneously. But in that instant he didn't speak, which even *he* recognized as being rather uncharacteristic.

"Look at me not saying nothing." His fingers touched gently on his chest. "You're *sure* you ain't Italian? Maybe you got a great uncle somewhere." He was teasing, of course, as we had been through all the differences in our backgrounds many times before. But there was also an edge of seriousness.

"I got uncles, Paulo," I grinned at him, " but they're all named Weinstock and LeVine and Hornstein."

"You going to write about me some day?"

"You sound like you'd like it." We both had heard the plaintiveness in his tone.

"You want to know what I was thinking just now?" Paulo leaned forward and cradled his forehead between his thumb and index finger. It had been eight months since that hand had been engaged in work. "I was thinking sometimes when you come and talk to me, it makes me feel like I'm living in some peasant village in Italy, not that I remember any peasant village. It just seems that way. You come, like you were some tourists; looking at the buildings and the churches, studying the faces of people, you know what I mean. Then it's like you want to take a picture of me, like for a souvenir, although I know that's not what you do this for. I think, the guy wants to be my friend even though he's just passing through. I suppose I think that 'cause you don't live here. I think of all the ways we're different and why it is we're so different. Money isn't the only thing. Then I think, he wants a picture, why not give it to him. Okay, I say, you can take my picture. You can even have somebody else take a picture of the two of us together, if that's what you want. Maybe you'll remember me better that way. After all, it isn't your fault I have to live like this and you get to move in and out of this peasant town. Besides, *you* want a picture of *me*, and that's got to mean something, don't it. What the hell, if you give me a copy, I'll have a souvenir of you, a reminder of what I looked like too, when

I was with you that time. Like I say, all the problems we face ain't your fault. Maybe they're nobody's fault."

"And if I want to show the picture to other people?" I interrupted him.

"That's *your* business. If you think they might be interested, you can even sell them for all I care. I'm satisfied with a picture. It makes me know I'm alive. Tourist or not, you wanted a picture and you picked me. You'll forget me two days later, remember me for two days when you get the film back, then forget me again."

"You think it goes like that, Paulo?"

"I think it goes like that for millions of years. Millions of people have lived their lives with no one paying an ounce of attention to them. Some of them like it that way. Some of them probably don't even think about people in other villages, not to mention tourists. But people like me, we're overlooked by the people who live ten feet away. Settle for a photograph? I'll settle for a wink if it means I might get the slightest break. Drink your coffee. Wait too long and it loses its poison."

In many respects, this conversation with Paulo Marcucci touches upon the concerns of this book. For the last ten years I have been speaking with people who are mainly from the poorer reaches of American society. My research consists of nothing more than these conversations. There is no telling how any one morning, afternoon, or evening might go, for I bring no prearranged questions, no structured form of interview schedule. It is a conversation in which I am engaged, or an event in which, in one form or another, I participate. I enter these conversations and events knowing that I will be observing others as well as observing myself observing them in a manner I normally do not assume. Thus, there is something unusual for me about these so-called observant participations, in that I anticipate doing more with the experience than merely letting it pass into time. In a sense I am a photographer prepared to take photographs, aware that each photograph will be a subjective response to what I am seeing and hearing. I *could* claim that I render authentic, objective portraits of people like Paulo Marcucci, but I recognize that I am presenting nothing more, nothing less than my impression, my slant, ineluctably my bias. In the portraits and studies that constitute this book, I, along with the other participants, provide our own reading of the social and personal situations in which we find ourselves.

In the past, the phrase that best characterized this type of work was observant participation. This is not merely a play on words of the well-known participant observation technique; by transposing the words, the stress falls on participation rather than observation. A better phrase might be observant implication, for the interviewer cannot help but become immersed in the lives of those people whom he or she is interviewing. This is one of the central issues of this book. The following studies convey small pieces of life as it is led and described by people with whom I have spoken. More generally, they focus on the ways in which people read the historical and contemporary situations of their lives, and what they perceive as their fate.

No one who listens to people recounting these situations can possibly remain aloof, indifferent, and still communicate his or her interest to the story tellers. We are not engaged here in classical psychoanalytic psychotherapy in which analysts purposely arrange for their patients not to see their faces. These are conversations, like the one with Paulo Marcucci in a noisy coffee shop; a conversation with a friend, albeit a special friend, who looks at me with myriad expressions, one of which clearly evinces a concern that I may be losing interest in him.

Paulo Marcucci is not unique in his attitude toward the hypothetical man in the downtown office who cares little for the Paulo Marcuccis of the world. Paulo's observation no doubt is correct. The hypothetical man aside, few countries pay much attention to their poor families. Governments proceed with their master plans or, more likely, their bureaucratic inefficiencies and minor reform programs, relying on the fact that the poor will start no uprisings. As Paulo said, most people believe that the lives of the poor and working class are dull, that their minds are vague, their outlooks and problems uninteresting, unoriginal. In my conversations with people like Paulo, again and again I have heard the sentiment, "I don't know what anyone would find so interesting about us." But their concern in these moments is with me, the interviewer, the somewhat irreal friend. It is me they doubt, for I represent the society that holds them back, the society that finds them of minimal interest and value. They wish to talk about certain

matters, but they are always alert to any clues that might suggest disinterest on my part.

Strangely, as the years of these special conversations accu-
mulate, I discover this sentiment in a great many people, not
merely those from the so-called lower reaches of society. Celebrities aside, many people doubt that someone else could be
interested in them. Admittedly, there are good and obvious
reasons for people living in poor circumstances to doubt the
intentions of someone like myself who claims to be interested
in them. A history of political and economic realities stands
between us. As best as it can, society segregates the poor and
leaves them to survive with one another. But there is no com-
parable history standing between me and others from higher
social strata with whom I speak. So with all people, one must
resolve the issue of mutual trust.

There is also the matter of examining the currencies that
each of us is putting in and taking out of these conversations
and friendships. What do I want from them? What is it they
want and do not want from me? Although for different reasons, sociologists and the people with whom I speak share one
fundamental concern about this form of inquiry: they wonder
how my work can consist of little more than conversing and
writing up these conversations. While some professionals argue
that further analysis of the material must be undertaken, the
people with whom I converse are convinced that I must have
some greater purpose in mind, one that transcends the writing
of a book. Surely, they say, it is not merely an interest in them
that could dominate the work; I must be using them as illus-
trations of something.

There is another issue about these conversations that assumes significance. It regards the protection of personal privacy. The matter of simultaneously wanting to write about
the lives of those with whom one speaks while preserving their
dignity and privacy is a delicate one. At all stages of one's
work, it poses a dilemma for the researcher. On the one hand,
I strongly believe that it is essential to record the lives of human beings as accurately and systematically as possible, and
that when one's so-called recording devices are subjective, they
be labeled as such. On the other hand, recording the life of another person—which means recording only the smallest frac-
tion of that person's experiences and recollections of those
experiences—may well violate the sense of privacy a researcher

wishes to preserve. The dilemma is intensified by the fact that in American society, there is tremendous pressure to have people expose their private lives; the more outrageous the divulgence, the more we encourage and accept it. Divulgence even becomes a part of political ideology. People wish to make public confessions or have others confess to one thing or another. Under the banners of freedom of speech, liberation, and psychological health, come all sorts of pleas to have people open up and lay themselves bare.

For the most part, the large majority of sociological research does not do this. Indeed, the criticism often leveled at such work is that it hardly seems to touch on the private, and therefore meaningful—that ubiquitous word—parts of people's lives. The temptation to encourage disclosure of all varieties of private issues is always alive in the sort of work exemplified in this book. Many intimate questions might be asked, given the closeness of one's friendships with people. Many issues are talked about and could be publicly recorded.

It was with this dilemma in mind that the present book was conceived. I had participated in a series of conversations and events which actually had to do with the matter of privacy and personal revelations, as we will see in chapters 10 and 11. Part of the dilemma was resolved by making certain that the confidentiality of the participants was maintained. Thus I changed names and a few places, except of course when participants agreed that it was important to publicize their true identities. But in the main, the dilemma is never satisfactorily settled. For me, this remains one of the crucial ethical issues of this work, although obviously my decision about how to proceed has been reached. I have chosen to make public the lives of those willing to speak with me, people who agreed to have our conversations published. It should also be noted in this context that whenever possible, the participants read what I had written and were free to suggest deletions and changes in fact and tone.

One can argue indefinitely about the issues of public reporting and the preservation of privacy. One can assert, for example, that using only anecdotes from people's experiences preserves the dignity of these people more than would an extensive life study. Some would say it is better to present responses to attitude questionnaires or public opinion polls, for these measures generate all the information one needs, and in the process of collecting the information, one pays greatest respect to those providing the information. My own argument is that the so-called observant participation life study provides its own form of information which is no less valuable than the information accumulated through attitude questionnaires and polling. The information obtained in both sorts of inquiry is potentially valuable both in the formation of a social science and for the people participating in these studies.

Conversely, both objective and subjective studies may be of negligible value in the development of a science, and even harmful to the participants. Any piece of conversation that one reports, no matter how extensive and elaborate, is open to interpretation. For example, a life study is produced in which I attempt to portray an articulate, thoughtful, and intelligent, young black man who has been bused to a predominantly white suburban high school. I make no claims that other black children share the views of this one young man; indeed I make every effort to point out that the young man speaks only for himself. Nonetheless, a panoply of responses to the study comes forth. The young man is seen by some as typical, by others as perfectly atypical. Some believe that I have created the young man out of my imagination. Some say that I have derogated him by not portraying him as intelligent. Some wish to use the boy as a justification for busing school children; others use "the case" as a justification for their opposition to busing. Some claim it noble for a rich researcher to work with poor children; others claim the life study contributes to the oppression of the young man and others like him, and that writers grow rich on the backs of the poor. Some claim that rendering portraits of poor people in even a slightly artistic fashion automatically turns them into the proverbial noble savage, thereby convincing one's readers that these people, as attested to by the beauty and majesty of their words, require no special political or economic support. Finally, some contend that the truth must come from systematic studies and observations no matter how they are carried out; others contend that only artists record the truth.

All of these extremes, naturally, are dangerous and to a certain extent are expressed with little thought given to their meaning and implications. Still, the dilemma of preserving privacy while publicly recording the way lives are led is unresolved and will remain unresolved in this book, although my own bias on the matter is clear. The issue, furthermore, raises one of the central ethical questions inherent in such work:

what is involved in participating in conversations when, through the definition of the situation, one is distinct from the other person in very real ways? (Paulo Marcucci will not write a book about his conversations with me.) Facing this question forces one to totally reassess the nature of one's work. Should the researcher continue the enterprise when maintenance of genuinely ethical relationships is so difficult, particularly when the substance of these conversations is personal and meaningful for all participants? My own answer, again, is clear, for I have chosen to continue the work believing that the alternative, namely to turn away from the people with whom I have been speaking, is unthinkable.

Now, why unthinkable? Several reasons may be offered which hopefully will add to our understanding of the purpose of this volume. Let me begin to answer the question by proclaiming a philosophy of living I strongly support but cannot seem to follow: live life every day, as if that day were the last day of your life; take in as much as you can, for there is so much to be gained, so much to be lost. The spirit of this philosophy appeals to me, but a laziness intervenes. I do lose too much each day, and confess to existing as if an endless stretch of time lay before me. But there is also a political side to the philosophy, for it assumes that each of us, no matter what his station in life, may live each day with a spirit of insatiable adventure and a delight in simply being alive. Looking for scraps to eat, or waiting in line at a welfare or unemployment office would seem to make it difficult to adhere to the spirit of the philosophy. Still, there is something significant about the idea of not losing human experiences. This is what strikes most intensely in my participation with others. I visit a city and want to walk down every street; I meet a person and want to know everything about him or her. The restraints on satisfying these needs are obvious, and as much as anything I feel the rush of time. How much longer will I stay with Paulo Marcucci while he is in this special mood? How much longer will he allow me to remain friends with him?

The result of this feeling is a desire to record conversations and ensure that our agreements, our contracts, really, regarding our work together will not be violated; that I will not reveal what someone has asked me to hold in confidence, but that I will also not allow those rare moments of our involvement to pass unrecorded. In other words, I feel that these conversations are as important as the daily events one reads about in newspapers. For, a constant source of information about and awareness of the men and women in our society is better than a communication system that will dehumanize, categorize, generalize, and make pronouncements about us that reveal neither the truth nor the substance of our lives. I despise the fact that our society encourages people to dwell on the sexual habits of famous men and women and then turns this encouragement into big business. Similarly, I reject the belief that the worlds of quiet men and women must go unnoticed or be treated strictly as actuarial or statistical concerns. Lives are recorded because there is inherent value in preserving human experiences, especially those experiences which for political and economic reasons are deemed "less significant" and "less profitable." Let us not forget, as Paulo Marcucci suggested, that economic criteria of success and failure too often influence the assessment we make of our own and other people's fundamental worth.

There is a second reason for recording these conversations: like it or not, American society thrives on the dehumanizing marriage between technological genius and a driving materialism demanding continuous acquisition. We want more homes and cars; we demand more and more information of any variety, no matter how seriously we violate our moral precepts. Little we do seems to affect this current. Some of us also formulate policy that dictates the ways people should lead their lives. We put into operation programs that directly or indirectly affect the lives of all human beings. All societies and governments do this. Rules and laws are inevitable components of social order.

Thus, underlying the acquisition of material goods and knowledge and the surge to design programs and policies, is a dehumanization that already has taken hold in Western culture. It is a dehumanization that we now accept, expect *and* justify. In our press for knowledge in the form of tangible certainties and in our fear of tentativeness and doubt, we actually believe we know what other people need and want, the ways in which they should seek gratification, and the scientific reasons supporting all of this. Social scientists actually claim to understand the mysteries of child development and the emergence of personal capacities, both cognitive and emotional. We claim to understand the workings of the human mind and spirit; hence we believe that we can write our policy statements and support them with knowledge about men and women whose lives we never encounter. Indeed our information and the theories generated from it are so sophisticated, we decide it is actually better to make claims about people we know little about, for in this way our decisions "prove" less biased. We claim to know about children because we have them, the elderly because we have a few older relatives still alive, minority people because we are minority people ourselves, or have spoken to some minority people, or because some of our best friends. . . . So it comes to pass that some of us have earned the right to speak for other people and to claim that we know what it is they want.

The truth is, however, that no one literally speaks for anyone else. One may have earned the right to create policy, or politically represent a constituency. But speaking for someone else is at best a compromise and a convenience, if not an outright presumption, no matter how legitimate a political act it may be. Because isolation breeds dogmatism and righteousness, the best way to know that one's notions, theories, and suppositions are right may be to take them to the people about whom they were originally conceived. Well, goes one argument against this position, most people don't really know *what* they want. Moreover, says another argument, it is difficult to look someone in the eye when writing a policy that one knows is barely a stop-gap measure. It is far more difficult to make claims about people you choose to be with every day of your life than it is to isolate yourself and make your claims, almost hoping that those whose lives you are addressing will never hear your remarks.

A literary critic once wrote that we don't need to know any more about people; we need policy. It is a familiar refrain. One can argue this position by saying that certain policies have hurt people far more than research projects purporting to study them. What we need, the argument would continue, is a world free of policies, one that truly honors and protects people.

But there is a more subtle argument to the critic's pronouncement. We focus on the word "know" because, in this context, it implies that we already possess all the necessary information on a particular subject of human behavior. That is quite an accomplishment for the social sciences! The word "know" implies something else as well. To know something is not merely to acquire still another material possession. Knowing how to speak a second language is not equivalent to purchasing a second house. To know something and to retain and elaborate on the original experience of the knowledge is a timeless adventure and ordeal. We do not know about poor children and working-class children merely from the type of brief accounts to be presented in Section Two of this book. From these accounts we will learn a bit, in a material sense, for we will become "acquainted" with the lives of a few more people. That is, we will elaborate on our existing knowledge. We also will *feel* this new knowledge, since the lives of these boys and girls will evoke in us unpredictable reflections and emotions. Said differently, knowledge may represent, in a shorthand sense, the accumulation of wholly impersonal information. More likely, it is itself an experience, containing its attendant emotional lights and shadows. That the emotional aspects, the feeling part of knowledge, may not be conscious to us—using one terminology—or cognitively salient to us—using another terminology—does not mean that this part is absent.

We said earlier that no one can listen to the accounts of another person's life and remain indifferent or objective, particularly when one is a part of the situation or friendship that has created and perpetuated the conversation. Inevitably, something is evoked in us: our mind is turned to other subjects; or we feel moved; or a particular emotion comes over us that we either cannot identify or choose to ignore. All of this is part of routine conversation, the act of preparing a life study, and accumulating new knowledge. Thus, we may turn the critic's words around slightly with the following statement: While politically it may seem that policy is more beneficial than the enlightenment or evocation derived from still one more life study, the fact is that in the end, policies may not be better. Yet, productive or destructive, policies do make it easier for us to deal with people when we do not wish to be touched by their lives. Writing policy is much easier than looking into someone's eyes as he or she reveals even the smallest morsel of himself or herself. No doubt there are times when preventing participants in psychoanalysis from seeing one another allows them to speak freely. But this method helps the analyst as well, for there are moments when he or she winces or weeps while listening to patients, and does not wish to burden the patient with such responses; or perhaps the analyst does not want to admit to having been so moved, and to having felt so helpless.

The word helpless brings us to another aspect of the response of many people to the life study. Reading the words of another person or the accounts of some events (as, for example, those presented in Section Four) creates a burden of which psychologists are well aware. What are we to do with this morass of words, this conversation just "overheard"? Are we to analyze it, place its words into some tradition of understanding that we find congenial? Are we to use these words, these lives, these events to shape political programs? Or are we to be merely entertained or informed?

Everyone responds differently to the words of another person. As the life study makes plain, what we know about another person, what he or she gives to us in conversation and friendship, is in great measure that person's response to *us*. We ourselves are the agents of information; people give us what they believe we want or assume we are willing to accept. Thus, our claims about another person may be unjustifiable, because we know only what that person has communicated to *us;* we do not know how this person would be heard and perceived by anyone else. Nor do we know what this person would tell anyone else. We may say that our work is phenomenological in nature, that people are offering to us freely their recounting of their private world or some public event. But just as thought and language have their social components, so too is the fundamental nature of the account and the art of recounting a sociological event, based on ritual and the laws governing simple routines. We, the listeners, are part of these rituals and routines. To say, therefore, that during our conversation Mr. X was putting on an act, is to say only that the normal and expected act of conversation and recounting was accentuated beyond normal, expected limits. But all social engagements imply actors acting, in a literal sense, a factor which in no way automatically renders disingenuous the act of recounting conversation.

The point has been belabored, perhaps, but it must be underscored. The richness, the depth of recounting conversation is lost if we say, simply, that there are environmental factors to consider. There are always environmental factors, but part of the environment is the invisible sociological realm of habit, routine, order, ritual, sharing, and everything else that constitutes the context of conversation. Variations in the rituals always exist, but the listener also creates some of these variations. To a degree that can never be accurately calculated, I, the researcher, determine the phenomenology and expressions, and hence, the personal accounts of those people I study. Even when I claim that I have done little, said little, allowed the other person to speak freely about whatever it is he or she wanted to speak about, my presence can be detected in the utterances of that person, just as their utterances will be found in my writing.

This last point may be developed further. First, the degree to which I, as researcher, choose to analyze the accounts of another person, literally his or her words, indicates not only something about the form of science or type of inquiry I am undertaking, but also something about my attitude toward those I study. I choose how much of the other person's presence I want to make public in my own accounting of his or her accounts. There is a great difference, after all, between merely saying that someone was talking to me about politics, and actually presenting the words of that person. Each way of recounting has its greater and lesser degrees of validity, its greater and lesser likelihood of recording the truth, subjective as it is, of a particular account. In the end, how many words of another person I include in my account suggests the value of those words in the act of performing my research. The words and the presence in the environment of both partici- pants, the mutuality of the conversation—no matter how asymmetric the relationship of the participants—is part of the truth one consciously is choosing to present.

To repeat, we are always recounting life experiences *in proc- ess.* We are involved with private lives and public accounts; nothing and no one will hold still long enough for us to de- scribe them perfectly and accurately. The world changes and changes us, even as we make our observations and recordings. Beyond this inevitable limitation of our science, our observa- tions and perceptions necessarily are personal and subjective, if we are making accounts or listening to accounts of life as it unfolds. But note again the stress on the word accounts. Peo- ple are telling us what happened, what crossed their minds, what they recall. What we are hearing is a tertiary elaboration of the original experience. Paulo Marcucci's *remembrance* of an event is one step away from living the event itself, as the event originally was experienced. Another elaboration is my hearing him tell of the event. My writing of the event yields still another elaboration. And all of these complicating mat- ters belong to what we call the environment of a conversation.

Another point about the environment of the conversation involves the question of whether or not the presence of the researcher should be recorded in the final account. Is there a legitimate place in the recounting of speech for dialogue of the type presented at the beginning of this chapter? On the one hand, this matter raises serious methodological issues. On the other hand, the answer one chooses comes down to a matter of taste. Some people want to know what the researcher said and did, and particularly what was going through his or her mind during the conversation. Others argue that the researcher's utterances and reflections only get in the way and keep us from hearing what the person under study is saying.

Whether it is explicitly or implicitly drawn, the presence of the researcher is in the conversation, in the environment, and in the final accounting of the conversation. There is no escape from this fact, other than to disregard the conversation and conceptualize about human behavior as if one could not remember the source of one's insights. Asthetically, it may trouble some readers to "hear" the researcher's insights, reflections, even words said in the course of conversation. But these insights and reflections, these words assuredly will influence the recounting, whether they are reported or not.

Reporting one's own contributions to conversations also affects that evocative aspect of knowledge acquisition mentioned earlier, although its effect on the reader is unpredictable. For some people, that which is evoked is enhanced by the researcher's participation. For other people, the obverse is true. Either way, the reader's reactions are formed partly in response to whether or not he or she wishes to identify with the presence of the researcher, or the so-called subject of the conversation. Upon reading a fictional account, the reader may say that it was like actually being there. In the social sciences, the feeling of "being there" is often taken as a sign that true science has not been made; it reads too personally to be pure science. More importantly, one wonders whether the reader of the account does not share something of the qualities of the researcher; both, in a sense, are part of the environment that has shaped the conversation.

A word now about the limiting nature of the environment in which the private life and public account unfold. I administer a test of intelligence to a child. I score the test, and the child's result is 90. I contend that on the basis of this measure, the child is not intelligent. Someone else administers an intelligence test to the same child, who now scores 120. The other examiner claims that the child is highly intelligent. The difference in the scores is not accounted for merely by the fact that it was the child's second testing. The difference is in part due to the environment and the examiner. The range of people's behavior, capacities, and propensities is enormous, far more expansive than we normally acknowledge. Yet these ranges are finite. People cannot become totally different organisms or personalities as they pass from one relationship or situation to another; they must maintain some semblance of self-consistency to retain their health and sense of identity. Thus, we offer different parts of ourselves, with greater or lesser intensity, to different friends and associates.

How then do we make science from all this? How can we claim to know about people? How do we even know that the parts of one's personality that one exposes, or the experiences that one relates, are the most important parts? At times, the stranger, the interviewer, or psychotherapist, becomes the recipient of some of the most tender, raw, and intimate material. After making some revelation, the teller claims surprise, disbelief over what has been revealed, and may hope that he or she will not have to see the interviewer again. In psychotherapy, the patient's demand for intimacy before revelation is frequently transformed into a demand for a guarantee of no intimacy before divulging intimate material.

This point too must be underscored, for it touches upon yet another question of the life study; namely, who, ultimately, is best qualified to do this work? Who, in the end, is entitled to participate in these special conversations? Can men interview women, whites interview blacks, older people interview younger people? The question is crucial, for it raises political and methodological issues, as well as issues of how we respond in terms of action to hearing accounts of other people's lives. It also raises the issue of whether or not the life study should include the reactions and responses of the interviewer during the original conversation.

A discussion of these issues must start with acknowledging the fact that any personal expression, even one that occurs symbolically, as in a dream, reflects more than the personality or the phenomenological apparatus of a person. We may wish to believe that each utterance, or at least some of our utterances, are purely our own, conceived by us in the twinkling of a moment. The fact is, however, that deeply rooted cultural and social structural forces influence these expressions and utterances, even the symbolic expressions associated with daydreams and fantasies. Paulo Marcucci's likening of our conversations to my taking his photograph in a peasant village neither one of us has ever visited, demonstrates this point. A sudden notion comes into his head, an image which not only depicts the predominating quality in our relationship, but also reveals the arrangements of power, economic realities, and the circumstances of our respective lives. While we may choose to overlook the forces of our culture and our society—as we typically forget the effect of the structure of our language on our thoughts—these forces emerge in our daily expressions, particularly when our expressions are made to someone who comes to us wanting to hear about the circumstances of our lives.

When, as researchers, our intention is to record the way life is led by anyone, not merely representatives of special portions of society, we necessarily will hear about and experience the affect of the social structure on the most innocuous or the most intimate details of that life. This is a fact of life. For we are not only bound by propensities that are biologically determined. We are also social animals in the sense that our public and private behaviors, as well as our accounting for these behaviors, are influenced by the values, norms, rituals, and structures of the world in which we survive. A personal diary, recording, novel, poem, in which a person divulges the most intimate and sensitive material, will necessarily reveal social structural qualities. Art is never free of them; it doesn't need to be in order to be considered art. The inner world may be distinct from the outer world, that which we call the unconscious distinct from the conscious. But interior worlds relate to exterior worlds, the unconscious touches on the conscious, and all realms of the mind along with public behavior "know" and "feel" the impress of the culture in which these realms evolve.

Many people demand that the life study include the influence of social and cultural forces when recording even the most idiosyncratic experience. A legitimate criticism of the life study is that it often may not make explicit what is implicit. It must be remembered that not only will oral history reflect social structural forces, but that these forces are at work in every conversation in which the oral history is born and matures. Merely to converse is to be involved in a process governed by social structural as well as psychological factors. All oral history necessarily reflects the relationship among politi-

cal, economic, religious, educational institutions, and patterns
describing the way a single life is led. We may allege that our work is little more than a monologue or dialogue, the recording of one man or woman speaking about his or her life. But this so-called free monologue is colored by exterior influences that transcend even the patterns of thought and behavior laid down by the language one is speaking. To make the monologue a dialogue, as all interview situations are, is to make more complex the social reality and accounting of the dialogue by both participants, and to set the conversation even more securely within the province of the sociological enterprise.

Any conversation, any accumulation of information through interviewing, will have political overtones or undertones. Again, Paulo Marcucci's reference to photographs is apt. The subjective recording of a conversation is a series of still photographs, in contrast to a recording on film or tape of that same conversation. Each segment of the conversation, each photograph lives in the memory of each participant. The memory, however, is the negative, not the photograph. Presumably, all of the conversation has been retained, but not all the potential photographs will be developed or publicly displayed. Moreover, each photograph, each segment of recollection, the souvenir, in Paulo's words, must then be developed individually. It is in the developing process that the personal, social, and political elements of the photographer-recorder will begin to emerge.

Let us recall, although the metaphor is not wholly justifiable, that just as two people will photograph the same event or person differently, so will two people develop and print the same photographic negative differently. One person will emphasize one quality of the photograph, the other will emphasize something else. In this personal emphasis, in this final artistic rendering—the period when editorial and substantive changes are made—lies the heart of the subjective inquiry, which is what the life study and the accounting of public and private experience is ultimately about. We choose only certain photographs, select only certain portions of a particular conversation, remember only certain fragments of conversation. It has to be this way, even with mechanical recording devices. Data, no matter in what form, are reduced. The reduction process is a linear one, and it is an inevitable one. We cannot remember everything; we can only report what happened in linear fashion. Photograph follows photograph, one by one, in the same way that words follow each other, one by one. In this linear process of memory, in choosing what to tell of our experiences—which is what both participants in a conversation must do—political, social, psychological influences again have an impact. In the final product, we may choose either to present these influences in an explicit manner, or to mask them. Thus, our product, the life study, may be so subtle in its political message that we, the creators of the message, may not recognize the politics of our work until others point it out. Conversely, our political message may be explicit to the point of our product becoming polemical. Either way, to some extent the life study remains ideological, never value free. Indeed, some who practice the method of observant participation depend on the ideological basis of the work, and rejoice in the work's explicit political content.

Now then, can a member of one distinct social group, one sex, engage in the sort of relationship required in the life study, with members of other groups, or people of the other sex? Obviously they can, and they do. Typically, we rarely question the premise that a man may tell another man things he would never tell a woman, or that a woman would reveal things to another woman that she would never tell a man. Yet, research indicates that in truth, male patients tell female therapists many things they have told no other person, and female patients reveal to male therapists the most private chapters of their lives. To be sure, a person may prefer to speak to an older man, or a younger woman, or a white man, or a black woman, or a professional person, or a distinctly nonprofessional person. But what ultimately emerges in the conversation is the expression of the participant in the context of political and social factors prevailing at the moment of the conversation *and* at the moment of the final recording of that conversation.

To understand human behavior and to enhance human life —which are the goals of the type of inquiry we are considering here—we must know the full range of human interactions. There are sound intellectual and political reasons why members of a particular group or sex prefer to remain with their own kind and speak of their private worlds only to one another. One reason is due to the oppression and exclusion certain groups of people experience daily. This experience testifies to the fact that we have not made much progress in dealing with

people who, on the most superficial level, appear different
from us. Apart from, or perhaps because of political inequali-
ties, some men are edgy with women, some whites are edgy
with blacks. Even a six-year-old child may appear diffident in
the presence of a toddler. As Erik Erikson wrote, we often
look at one another as if we were representatives of various
species or subspecies, not sure whether our perceived—not to
mention imagined—differences affirm the greatness of life, or
anticipate our demise in a battle among the species. The differences between us evoke a need to articulate what it is that
constitutes the boundaries and substances of our private and
public selves. What we decide about these boundaries and substances is found in our accounts, privately and publicly recorded.

When people of similar backgrounds, so-called similar human categories, participate in the life study, the political and
social contexts shift. To say, however, that these sorts of interactions are more genuine, more likely to reveal the truth
than are interactions between people of different backgrounds,
is a perplexing matter. It is merely that at certain points in
history, our intellectual, political, and psychological needs
make demands upon us and teach us to value one form of research, one life study, more than another. The oppressive
elements existing in a society will necessarily influence the
science practiced by members of that society. These same elements will appear as well in our conversations and observant
participations.

By the same token, blind spots also will appear in our conversations, sometimes because we are victimized by the political and social realities of our culture, sometimes because we
believe that we are immune to the pressures of these realities.
This is particularly true when we do nothing more than speak
with another person and record bits of this experiential history. Political ideology supports us, drives our work, lingers
in the air above us, settles in the ground beneath us. It also
blinds us from time to time. We begin to make claims about
people and speak for them in ways that conceal the truths of
their existence and corrupt the images and remembrances we
have of these people and their circumstances. Thus, in our observant participations, we face the dangers of romanticizing
people. We can be condescending, personally self-indulgent,
irresponsible, patronizing. We also can be ideological to the
extent that we convince ourselves and those with whom we

participate that we are doing the "right thing," acting in the "right way."

The so-called raising of conscious awareness of human circumstances is one of the main intellectual goals of the life study. We must learn about people, and feel through their words, or their words married to our words, the substance of their lives. Making policy, as we noted earlier, is a different enterprise altogether. But by engaging in conscious and explicit polemics, we often end up in the same position as those who write policy. The danger exists if we ignore certain facts of another person's existence and merely employ that person's words as grist for our mills of ideology and power. Like policy formation, the preoccupation with ideology may prevent us from feeling what another person has told us, or better, wishes to tell us. We may believe we are being our "most human selves" when we grab onto others who seem similar to us, and urge them to express what is on their mind. But in these instances we run the risk of merely offering different sets of constraints, different definitions of freedom.

In the end, one is left believing that there are good life studies and not such good life studies. Some studies genuinely honor human life, the circumstances that govern and provide contexts for that life, as well as the recounting of it. Some work also enhances the lives of the participants. How one evaluates the type of work we have been describing will not be addressed in this volume. We can say, however, in light of our previous discussion, that these evaluations will be as subjectively rendered as the life study itself, and influenced by the same political and social structural realities. On the matter of enhancing human life through the type of work one does, a brief remark may be offered.

No one can say authoritatively what sort of social scientific inquiry ultimately will enhance human life. Hundreds, perhaps thousands of now faceless men and women spent millions of hours cultivating molds in petrie dishes. The results of their individual efforts may seem small, but the methodological tradition of the inquiry lead to Fleming's discovery of penicillin. There is, of course, the serendipitous discovery, but it always is grounded in a well-established, often effete-appearing tradition.

One cannot predict what people will do with the accumulation of words that constitute the accounts of private lives and public experiences. As we remarked earlier, the same data can be used to justify wholly antithetical intellectual and political perspectives. Regarding the life study, there is no guarantee that the information one collects is of greater or lesser value, as judged by any set of criteria, than the information accumulated through other equally tentative and imperfect methods.

Clearly, no one method alone will ever constitute a science. As a personal note, however, the method we call observant participation, the rendering of a life study, seems to be congenial to those researchers who prefer to "photograph" people and situations in more natural settings. Such researchers do not fit into the social-psychological harness required to perform other sorts of interpersonal inquiries. They are unlike those researchers who make their inquiries into human behavior by staying as far away from people as they can, or at least by ensuring that the social situations in which they make their inquiries are free of genuinely personal exchanges and sharing. Right or wrong, these investigators claim that the sort of mutual recognition and the friendship upon which the life study is predicated, would contaminate their investigation and distort their results. Their contention well may be true. For scientific, psychological, and political reasons, there are times when some human beings label and treat other human beings as research subjects, guinea pigs. Their involvement with their subjects is highly circumscribed, and in many instances, presumably, justifiable. But in undertaking the life study, many of the principles and ethics of the so-called laboratory experiment are irrelevant and inappropriate.

This book is not a collection of manipulations with experimental subjects. However, no research can totally avoid human manipulations of one sort or another. In simplest terms, the researcher possesses a special power; he or she maintains ultimate control, although manipulations work both ways. Nonetheless, I prefer to regard the present volume as a series of conversations with friends. These conversations, as I have stated, are never free of the influence of political and social realities. Whether or not my own words from the conversations are included, my sentiments, feelings, and politics could not be more in evidence.

As for whether or not the following studies enhance life, one cannot say. Partly, it is too soon to tell which one of the petrie dishes with which we presently work in the social sciences may lead to some valuable method, insight, or theory. Partly too, what one does with and for one's friends is not necessarily relevant to the recording of the accounts of lives. It is appropriate to suggest, however, that the researcher's attitude toward someone he or she calls a friend, is likely to be different from the researcher's attitude toward someone he or she calls an experimental subject; again those social structural realities that so strongly influence our private beliefs and tastes. Different sets of ethics develop from these two styles of research, along with characteristic perceptions, emotional responses, and definitions of the relationships and situations in which participants find themselves. An experiment has a finite stopping point, a logical, possibly even predetermined instant of conclusion. A life study has no such ending point, except for death. The conclusion of a particular experience or event does not imply the termination of a relationship.

There is another difference between these two types of research, one which Paulo Marcucci also perceived: the life study thrives on the dynamics of memory, recollection, remembrance. In an almost sentimental mood, as in the example of the tourist snapping photographs in an Italian peasant village, the entire enterprise rests on the concept of the souvenir, the tangible present holding tightly to an intangible past. Memory calls forth the material which is then processed and presented. The researcher then goes away, and in his or her ideological, psychological, intellectual contexts, creates a final statement, a piece of work. Here memory acts again, as recollections of recollections take form and come together as a subjective recording of private lives and public accounts. The tangible product in this instance is a book, a souvenir for the participants, a testimony, a statement of belief in the value of preserving human life through daily encounters and friendships.

I realize now that when I say my values or attitudes have changed over the years, it usually means that my current adult perceptions have little in common with my childhood perceptions of adulthood. It isn't exactly that my values have changed. Rather, how I imagined I would be as an adult, how I thought things worked, do not coincide with how my life actually is evolving. The practice of psychotherapy and, more appropriately, the conducting of research, help explain this "false change" in values.

As a boy hoping to become a doctor, I imagined that one did something with patients in private—a little something that had science and magic mixed together—and patients went away happy and well. Somewhere along the line I would be living pretty comfortably myself. One day a week, the fantasy continued, I would, as they used to say, give some time to charity. This meant working with poor people who, though they couldn't pay, presumably developed illnesses like the rest of us. Even as a child, I imagined charity work to be a less than private affair. It was open-ward and emergency-room work, on-the-street work, not small-sanitized-office work. There was another difference as well: you didn't talk much with charity cases. You performed a service, they thanked you and left, perhaps holding you in awe. Something else: you went to "their" part of the city, while your "regular" patients came to *you*.

The policy in many medical schools—as in the school I attended for one year—actually nurtured some of these fantasies. Third- or fourth-year medical students took off two weeks to deliver babies in poor communities. An uneasy balance was established between using these babies and their mothers for educational purposes, and providing doctors for families who could not afford them. What I heard from the medical students returning from these obstetric visitations was first, that they were nervous and didn't know what to do, and second, that the women who supposedly needed them had instructed them more articulately than had any professor. There was always the story, too, told with astonishment, of the woman with seven or ten kids who helped the doctor help her give birth, and four hours later was back cooking or scrubbing the kitchen floor. It was all incredible; the women, the families, the children, the neighborhoods. But in the end, it seemed that only a few students took away from these experiences the lasting idea of the strength, physical courage, and difficult conditions facing these families.

Childbirth was the exceptional moment, the unique case study. It was not viewed as yet another process that had to be endured within the tangible contexts of poverty. "Those people" were still out there, undernourished, having their babies without proper medical attention, and probably having nothing to do in their lives but *have* babies. No one considered their stamina or eloquence, only how gruesome it was where they lived and how much the women had helped them when they timorously entered those shabby homes. How in God's name was anything alive going to come out of that woman who, with her water burst and the baby practically crowning, had gotten up off a putrid-smelling mattress to open the door for the doctor?

During graduate training in sociology and psychology, I retained similar images about "those people out there," although "out there" was getting closer as the university was sprawling into those "out there" regions. These people were constantly being separated from us by one thing or another, and it wasn't always that ubiquitous creature, culture, that kept us apart. The question of how to study these people, reach them, and work with what our instructors told us, encouraged the separation.

Now here was a perplexing problem. The methodological techniques we were learning as young social scientists involved keeping data pure, free from anything that would "spoil" them. Indeed, one seemed to treat the data with greater antiseptic precautions than were taken by the doctors treating those mothers in labor. So we were learning the appropriate techniques of interviewing patients, clients, research subjects, and were being moved by these people, I suppose, but were not according them full human stature. When we got what we wanted, we immediately had to analyze it, interpret it, and wonder how much we could generalize about human behavior from what these people had said. Gradually, the child who volunteered to be in our study, or the woman who consented to be interviewed, or the man who brought to us, to strangers, his anguish and overpowering sadness, became a case history, a representative of something.

When the interview was over, a discussion followed with a dozen other students who either had observed the interview through one-way mirrors or while hidden in the darkness by partitions. Then the term papers and examinations were written and someone recalled the depressed guy with the Italian

name who came in that dreary afternoon three months before, the one who had been labeled a "borderline."

"What the hell was his name? Whatever happened to him?
They hospitalize him?"

"Someone gave him three bucks and sent him home in a
cab!"

"You ever read Frieda Fromm Reichman on depression?"
someone would ask. "She's got this great thing about. . . ."
And then all of us were gone.

I oversimplify numerous aspects of my education when I
say that professionalization quieted my involvement with
"those other people." What seemed natural and straightfor-
ward, the regular sort of chat with a new friend, even if that
friend ran a pool hall or was found waiting in an emergency
room of a city hospital, was being discredited. Professionals,
we had learned, transcend these simple anybody-can-have-
them type of relationships. They learn how to initiate encounters without becoming implicated, in such a way that the data
they collect remain systematic, clean, analyzable. They learn,
moreover, the importance of collecting the kind of material
that someone after them can collect. Indeed, the notion of
scientific replication seemed to imply that material had to present itself to the next person exactly as it had presented itself
to us; otherwise, the investigation's validity, stability, and re-
liability would be questioned. And always at issue was the
importance of not becoming involved with those whom one
studied. (Strangely, and something I discovered later, some
people with whom I now speak in the course of doing research
face these same issues with me. As noted in the previous chapter, some take seriously the friendship we have established.
They are concerned about the material they provide me with
and wonder how they are performing "their part of the
bargain" and whether their contribution to the research is
adequate. Others, of course, see the relationship strictly in research terms. They receive nothing from our conversations and
can terminate our association at any time.)

It was professionalism, those unseen spirits of dogma and
tradition, that actually affected not only our cognitive appa-
ratuses, but our private impressions and aspirations as well.
Dogma and tradition dictated that psychology should be practiced in an office, in a tie and jacket, and of course a fee must
be charged, for one must never forget what Freud wrote about
the symbolism of payment. Sociological work, moreover,

must be pursued, for want of a more elegant phrase, from afar; afar and above, more likely. One had to be on top of situations, protected by one's understanding and analyses. Hunches and wonderings were appropriate only for accomplished elders who appeared to rely on intuition, when actually they leaned on all varieties of empirical findings.

This is not to say that there weren't moments of humanism. Such moments were spring showers, soft downpours lasting for so short a time that the flowers were barely moistened. But they helped. Once, for example, a class of sixty of us towering intellectuals was watching a movie of a social worker speaking with a schizophrenic child. The professor, an eminent psychoanalyst, was unable to budge our vision and make us see what the movie was depicting. We found transference, repressed rage, and condescension on the part of the social worker. The professor saw a woman kneeling down in order to make eye contact with a small boy. "And what do you think," he asked gruffly from a high podium, "when a person comes into your office who appears to be having a psychotic episode?" We answered drugs, intensive treatment, examination of the entire family, not just the "labeled patient." "You think," he corrected us angrily, "there but for the grace of God. . . ."

Actually, most of us had been thinking something like that. I remember after class how we joked that if we treated a psychotic person we would be thinking, I'm glad it's you, pal, and not me. So we were close enough to the "correct" answer, except that our prepuberty professionalism did not allow this thought to be expressed and become part of any living ethic.

In contrast to those who showered us with a gentle humanness were those professors of medicine—and this was in the 1960s—who actually reported to the dean the names of students carrying books of poetry in their lab coats. My own illicit package was the works of Wallace Stevens. Because they had never studied the dynamics of urban public schools, those medical policemen never learned that being reported to the dean is the critical incitement to rebel. Wallace Stevens was poignant, moving, but not yet influential in shifting values or determining that old values were not being sustained. I would draw on the poets later on, however, when I needed support for the type of inquiry many social scientists found meager, frail, and unmanly—the subjective.

Then there was the actual research work and psychother-

apy. Case reports, a form of literature that always stimulated
us, also served, I fear, as a form of divertimento rather than as a full-fledged symphonic form. Glimpses of patients were "better" than reading turgid prose. But, like our attitude toward those women in the poor neighborhoods, the case stud- ies were always teaching us to treat humanness with a con- trolled posture. I remember asking once about the personal and literary significance of referring to a woman by her psycho- neurosis, or having a letter stand for her identity. It was more than confidentiality being preserved, I said, when Dr. T. treat- ed the thirty-eight-year-old female Caucasian Miss L. The rep- resentation of a whole human being was being withheld.

The case study, in other words, although a blessed relief from purely theoretical and empirical writings, was offering up a victim in the very mode practiced in introductory anato- my examinations. Here a tray was presented to the student. A reddish wax had been poured in the bottom of the tray, and pinned to it with straight pins was a tiny chunk of flesh, blood vessel or, more tricky, a wholly unidentifiable object. Then, while the liberal arts graduates grumbled about the insidious- ness of encountering body parts desecrated in this way and uttered words like gestalt and neoimpressionism, the anatom- ical dandies searched their memories and found the secret words. In the bar after the examination, there was always talk about walking down the street and finding—how fortuitously —a lonely chip off of some poor fellow's epididymis, like the one on the red wax tray.

Case studies had a bit of that same effect on us. Instead of a slice of an epidydimis, we had a bit of anal aggression or a soupçon of schizophrenia. But the patient's—dare I say per- son's—whole life was never revealed. Nor for that matter was the therapist's life, or his or her remarks during the treatment. Out of the clear blue sky the thirty-eight-year-old female Cau- casian just began speaking and the invisible recorder-therapist began writing or transcribing. So people, social situations, and human engagements were coming at us in the most fragment- ed fashion.

I am not certain that those of us being socialized in this way could articulate such feelings at the time. But surely one of the major forces urging us to read novels we had either already read or always heard we should read, was the need to witness human relationships unfold in the esthetic, imaginative, and holistic ways in which they genuinely unfold. Although appealing, the case study seemed inadequate because it often lacked the fascination with a single human being, or the concern with life and death, history and evolution that novelists had portrayed for us. Frequently, even the demeaning "slice of life" peek at men and women that newspapers and magazines published under the label of "human interest story," was more telling of the way life truly was led. In a peculiar sense, the case study and not the novel was fictive.

During this period of training and early professionalism, a similar set of constraints was imposed on research. Here again people were not people, were not meant to be people, but instead were transformed into quantifiable units. We learned how to transfer people's responses to our questions onto IBM cards and then stuff the cards into the machine itself. We learned computer programming and how to clean the data and, alas, analyze it. The complexity, ambiguity, and richness of even the limited interviews I conducted, contrasted markedly with the linear beauty and quintessential order of the data as it appeared all categorized and analyzed in gorgeous printouts. In the first moments of inspecting the material from the computer, human behavior, in effect, was interpreted, understood. While someone beginning a practice in psychotherapy could not readily admit to this sort of reaction, the truth was that the computer did bring that proverbial order to that proverbial chaos, and the feeling was actually satisfying. For the moment, anyway, my reactions to those I was "studying" could be denied, especially in the light of such glorious scientific (looking) results.

The computer's effect on me was the constant separation of myself from the people I had studied, the very people whose utterances I had transformed into numerical coefficients. If anything, I was implicated in the IBM system, not in the lives of those people kind enough to complete my questionnaires, the people I acknowledged in the footnotes of professional articles.

Perhaps the most frustrating of all the principles I had learned in graduate school was the principle of interactive indifference. In the name of science and psychotherapy, one stood apart from one's "subjects" and "patients." One emphasized analysis or understanding and worshipped results and the usefulness and beauty of ideas and books rather than the spirit and everyday action that constitute human survival. Quotations from authors could be inserted in manuscripts when they illustrated something, or provided the reader with a bit of the therapeutic or research ambience. But long quotations, descriptions, or meanderings about one's *friendship* with someone was deemed inappropriate, unprofessional.

Something else. When one included in a manuscript, pages of conversations rather than mere snatches and anecdotes, the person written about was inevitably labeled a patient. When a psychotherapist talked to someone, particularly someone living in a poor community—like those mothers the medical students befriended for two weeks—then that someone became a patient. Even today, I find that no matter how many times I write that those with whom I speak have not come to me seeking psychological treatment, that in fact I went to them, many critics, well-meaning to be sure, label these people, patients. Why else would a professional therapist be speaking with them if not for purpose of treatment or change? To report what they say, the critics also argue, is not enough. One must *do* something with the people or with their words. Reveries, opinions, reflections, feelings, whatever anyone tells us during our visits to their homes must be transformed into one of the world's professional currencies. We have been instructed to abstract the findings and analyze the words, which means impose on them classical objective analytic criteria. Sadly, the myriad forms of subjective analysis that underwrite the type of research many of us perform, continue to remain invisible to those schooled only in objective forms of analysis.

Let me linger on the idea of people speaking for themselves and allowing their words to be the final product of research. Throughout my training, there was always a message that words had to be transcended, lifted onto some greater plane of human significance. Well and good, for the analysis of the written and spoken word has a long tradition, and among the cognitive operations of listening are coding, decoding, organizing, synthesizing, and other forms of interpretation. That these processes are a fundamental part of human exchange testifies to the necessity of transposing individual word units into categories of more comprehensive meaning.

But there is an important political point to be made as well. The words of patients, of poor people, of those mothers again, could not attain the highest level of significance to us because of the relationships we had established with these people and the status we had thereby accorded them and ourselves. This was the fundamental distinction that struck me, not during my years of training, but afterward. Good doctors must shoot for a greater ideal—the ideal of making science. Anything resembling literature—and certain forms of psychotherapy resembled forms of literature—was not deemed consistent with the scientific enterprise.

I believed this. I would love to be able to say that in my mid-twenties' sophistication I argued with professors on the nature of truth and untruth, and the experiencing of multiple realities. But I did not. Indeed, I remember idolizing a man who practiced several forms of psychotherapy and at the same time was an outstanding student of matrix algebra. The latter work I concluded, compensated for the airy and rarified activities of the former work. The latter work, moreover, stood squarely on the road to making science, whereas the former represented merely listening and responding—hopefully sensitively—to people.

For years the words of people, the forms of their survival, the substance of their everyday and everynight needs, activities, and wonderings loomed as data to dissect, material to be poured into the architectural forms of theory building and empirical analysis. Words by themselves counted for little, except that certain colleagues rather admired anyone who did a great deal of interviewing "in the field." To acquire reams of notes from conversations with "ordinary" people—we weren't, after all, anthropologists engaged in a year of field work in New Guinea or the Bush—was a demiaccomplishment. Furthermore, to follow the procedure of psychotherapists and social scientists of speaking with people week in, week out for years, seemed a valuable undertaking, although as I understand reactions to this type of work, it still wasn't considered science.

In time, I found there was a natural way to perform my work in the homes I had rightly or wrongly invaded. I described the lives of people I had come to know and let them speak for themselves. No conscious decision was made regarding the major forms of the work. When long passages of speech were recounted, it was simply because there was not much else to do.

The reader may question this approach. If someone has spoken about something that matters to him or her, why does this necessarily preclude analysis in the manner, for example, in which Freud performed it in his elegant and clearly literary case studies? The person's identity can be hidden, so what constrains the researcher from making further analysis?

The answer to this question rests partly in the contract one establishes with the people about whom one writes. It is a contract essentially of friendship, of mutuality, and not merely one of questioning and answering. It is a contract predicated on a request that persons share moments of their lives. Research of this type does not constitute psychotherapy. I go to people and they give me real as well as symbolic moments of their time. I go, moreover, to speak to *them*, not strictly to research a problem or gather material that might elucidate some greater issue of which that person is merely a convenient example. The person is not an informant in the sense in which anthropologists use this term. The person's life, or really the tiny fragments he or she gives *me*—for other fragments are given to other investigators—represent the entirety of the inquiry.

In the selection of conversations, naturally, all sorts of political, economic, moral, educational, or religious issues play dominant roles. No one can hide his or her biases, prejudgments, or the visions produced by professional training. No one can hide the fact that when research takes someone into neighborhoods of poverty, that poverty itself may emerge as the nonabstract hero (or antihero) of the final work. Still, these issues may not be paramount in the moment-by-moment conversations that constitute the research. The work is nothing more than talking and listening, having one's mind wander, sometimes in step, presumably, with the teller of the story, sometimes in counterpoint to it. To repeat, this is the quintessential aspect of this form of subjective inquiry: the interaction, the friendship, the mutuality, the encounter. This is why the actual words spoken become so important and why no further objective analysis is left to be undertaken. It is research based on esthetic judgments and human intuition, both fundamental ingredients of the dramatic or dramaturgic. One seeks to know how life is led.

Each of us senses the private inner sphere of human reality and what influences it, and the exterior sphere and what seems to affect it. Everyone senses the ways in which these two spheres shift so that their boundaries are at times indistinguishable, and how this shifting may result from changes in either sphere or in the interplay between spheres. Essentially, this interplay lies at the core of the subjective inquiry. I mention this notion of spheres so that no one will think I am arguing that nothing existing in the mind of one person can ever be known by (to) another. The subjective encounter underlying this research includes the interviewer-intruder who possesses an inner sphere which at all times is having impressions made on it by another human being and the environment of this other human being. The writings of philosophers, scientists, psychotherapists, and novelists ripple my mind as I write that all I know is what I experience in the mutual presentment of selves that constitute any encounter of which I am a part.

The work, then, is based more on paying attention than on interpretation and more on reaction than on abstract analysis. It is a sharing of lives in which the asymmetry established by dint of the original interview relationship is never fully righted. But always there are the words, the other person's and my own, and the exchange which must enter the research and the friendship as well. The dramatic quality of the interaction persists in all interactions, but it is especially salient here because of the nature of the friendship and its special purpose as established at the outset. For this reason I refer to myself not only as a friend of those who share their lives with me, but also as an intruder. This perception is also shared by psychotherapists and counselors, for the feelings of intrusion exist in the therapeutic alliance even though the patient or client seeks out the therapist precisely because the therapist's role allows for a degree of symbolic invasion.

I mention the dramatic aspect too, because it reminds us of the public and sociological parts of research and psychotherapy. When we speak of authentic engagements, we must consider the public, situational, cultural aspects of this authenticity. Events and processes outside our private selves contribute to the determination of the authentic. Physical as well as psychological settings shape encounters and the eventual presentation of authenticity to another and to oneself. Thus, description of these settings must also be included in the documents one writes about others.

Another problem is that too many of us are in touch with the world only through television, our patients, or those in our research projects. Retelling their stories makes it seem as if we were authentic travelers in the world. With good intentions we may support an argument by revealing what people have disclosed to us, but again I wonder whether this is a legitimate act. These people have not come to us or allowed us to enter their homes with the understanding that they are informants. It is the enhancement of their lives that we have promised, and while value may accrue from bringing their words to those who might otherwise never hear them, an equally enhancing gesture is to keep their secrets and respect their privacy.

An important political distinction underlies the preservation or violation of confidentiality. I notice that when we speak about poor patients, much is divulged and often, too, a name is dropped. Confidentiality is more likely to be preserved when patients are affluent. While the matter of therapists deferring to the wealthy, or patients deferring to their therapists is a serious one, it ought not mask the notion that even people seeking treatment must decide whether or not to reveal private matters. The decision to reveal oneself in therapy is based on trust, but trusting is not a purely psychological act. Sociological features of the relationship like ethnicity, age, credentials, economic background, and status contribute to one's willingness to trust. Social standing cannot be the basis on which practitioners and researchers establish the limits of confidentiality.

I have perhaps touched on these last points merely to remind myself of the precariousness of therapy and interviewing. I am preoccupied with the question of overromanticizing another person's life, just as some of us are preoccupied with the power of our work. We believe strongly that our writing, research, or forms of treatment bring out clients, bring our friends into the light, or indeed, make them come alive. Granted, it is often through someone's writing that we learn of some person or condition. It is also true that those we work with and befriend are very much alive when we are not in their homes, nor they in our offices. They may appear "larger than life" during the magical fifty minutes of therapy, but soon they are again shut out from us.

I return to the issue of professional training and the positivist brand of research and practice that it advanced. It supported a separation of people, an assumed hierarchy of human significances, a belief that people may properly be used for certain purposes and that these purposes are essentially good. To be sure, we dealt only with bits of roles when we dealt with others. But this fragmented and abstracted treatment of human beings gradually assumed a rational justification for us, if not a genuine scientific importance. It was good analyzing other people's lives, sifting through people on the basis of criteria convenient to us; it was good listening only for certain utterances or attitudes and letting the rest go by; and it was good presenting one's findings in the traditional forms that excluded personal expression and made the rendering of science preeminent.

There is, however, an esthetic form of doing research, practicing therapy, and describing one's experiences. It has not yet been fully explored by social scientists, for some of us still dress in scientific trappings and fear that our work may be moving nearer humanistic traditions. We are asked, is it fiction or nonfiction? We answer, the events are true, the conditions and the people are as real as the very days of their lives. Did we get permission from them? We did. Did we use tape recorders? Sometimes. And are these people our patients? No. All such inquiries are valuable, but none of them touches upon the crucial questions: Is what we are doing truthful? Is it respectful of the truths of the single human life as it evolves within a culture, within psychological and sociological spheres, and according to the constraints of history? Is it mindful of the truths of ourselves, and the space, time, and movement which are uniquely our own and subject to change because of the research or therapy we practice? Is it respectful of the truths of the conversation and civilization in which these brief life moments are exchanged, then ramified in the private and public spheres of ourselves and others? And finally, is it mindful of the fact that we cannot know directly the life of anyone but ourselves?

This last question haunts me, particularly when I see the aging computer printouts on my shelves along with the notes I have taken only hours ago on a conversation with a child. I find myself wanting to deny this undeniable principle of human reality. But then, to comfort myself, I will say the child does not wholly know me either, and at least in this one sacred realm we stand equal. So now we both might continue our work and our friendship from this ideal premise.

No doubt, the word premise has a precarious quality about it, the very quality that makes me uncomfortable about practicing therapy *and* doing the type of research I have been describing. One source of this precariousness lies in the nature of the role one assumes in establishing any premise for human engagement, or conversation. Surely, we are beyond thinking that playing a role is, by definition, inauthentic. Like pretending, playing is not automatically an inauthentic gesture; it is the role and the demands it makes that cause us, in our self-consciousness, to feel dishonest or incomplete. Understandably, different personalities are attracted by different role demands; some of these demands are found to be satisfying, some oppressive. No matter what we believe about therapy and research, an ideology of some sort dominates this work, and distinct levels of power underlie it. Forms of truthfulness and equality exist in both enterprises but so too do forms of deceit and inequity.

Once I thought I had resolved the conflict between truth and untruth in my work. Traditional methods of research, I decided, were inauthentic; contemporary styles of therapy that spoke of wholeness and authenticity were genuine and true. Later, still hunting for simple resolutions, I shifted attitudes and decided that the subjective inquiry yielded the truth in contrast to even the most humane styles of psychotherapy. With each change in attitude my feelings were also transformed. First I felt healthy doing therapy, then I felt healthy doing research. Then I concluded that an old personality trait lay behind my shifting dissatisfactions. The instant I felt halfway competent at something I lost interest in it and sought something new, using the earlier activity as a symbol of what I no longer valued.

Presently I have a new assessment of my work, one that overflows with conflict. There is truth and untruth, equality and inequality in whatever I do, and each moment brings new gratification and new concern. I am not now speaking of the phenomenon we all recognize, that one is a good therapist at one session and inadequate at the next. Rather the culture, its politics and economics, its values and styles of human transaction necessarily influence every assessment of one's work, every instant of one's therapy and research. I hear the sounds of ideology, power, manipulation in every encounter, in the same way, probably, that some people hear the words of angels or devils. At times, when I am able to muffle these sounds I feel the work to be glorious, and even presume to think I have really heard someone. But gradually the sounds become loud again and I resume questioning my efforts and wonder whether I have not been deceived, or worse, deceived someone else.

Denial was one of the important psychological terms we examined in graduate school; delusion, in all its senses, is the word I have used again and again with myself since embarking on a career. Have I created situations under the banner of humanism and enhancement of life, that in fact are convenient for *me* philosophically, intellectually, financially, politically, all ways? And do I therefore find in these exquisitely prepared situations only those gratifications, truths, and equalities, as well as frustrations, deceptions, and inequities that *I* am able to deal with, or safely agonize over? It must be this way because I do not experience the same hurts as those who are oppressed experience. Knowing their anguish only by report causes me to feel inauthentic no matter what feelings I conjure up in response to it. When one is directly confronted by the suffering of another human being, something in one's soul changes forever. From that time on laughter and crying take on a different meaning. But the fear persists that I encounter human beings according to premises convenient for me and with devices that protect *my* vulnerabilities as much as theirs.

I have not remained unchanged by the encounters that constitute my therapy and research work. At least two signs convince me of this. First, I now take greater personal risks, in subtle and not so subtle ways, than ever before. Something about risk suggests that my conceptions of life and death have been altered in the course of doing my work. The second sign manifests itself as a sadness mixed with anger, a disconsolateness tinged with outrage. I call it a depression, thinking that by labeling the mood it might magically disappear. Surely many events and long-standing experiences play a part in this depression. But whatever its cause, I feel it connected in some important ways to the psychotherapy and research I perform. And no matter how mightily I try to push it aside, it hangs on and makes me think I will never be free of it.

T here are many problems with capitalism, it has been argued again and again, problems that perpetuate the
cruel treatment of the powerless and poor by the powerful and rich. Tax loopholes, the process of inherited wealth,
and above all, private property are among the problems, indeed evils, of capitalism. The question one must address is this:
Can a democratic society emerge when people *own* the land,
own the tools and the industries, *own* those who labor for
them?

In the 1960s, a decade some point to as a period of genuine social revolution, capitalism came under brutal attack. At
the most moderate and sanguine professional meetings, one
heard references to changing the economic system, fighting
the laws of private ownership. America needs changing from
top to bottom, these professionals said. Money is the root of
all evil, and private ownership, the ground in which this root
grows.

But this is only part of the so-called social revolution, the
part that attracts the economically and politically minded.
There is another part that involves the psychologically minded.
This part too has as one of its founding principles an abhor-
rence of what one might call the ownership of psychological
property or, more simply, privacy.

It is peculiar, this psychological part of America's social revolution. It seemed to surface quietly enough, but gradually,
among a great hubbub about the importance of free expression, the release of the repressed, the necessity of being open
to everyone and to every experience, came a new cry! Let it
all hang out! To have private thoughts, private emotions, was
deemed as pathological as owning land, a cotton factory, or
company store while others went hungry, unclothed, unshel-
tered. Now at these professional meetings where everybody
agreed on the evils of capitalism, they were speaking of the
importance of spilling guts, baring souls, opening up fully to
one another.

New businesses developed from all of this, and a new professional cadre was born, seemingly overnight, to help the rest
of us uptight folks become downright loose. They were telling us, this new cadre, that even if it meant taking lessons or
traveling long distances to special resorts and retreats, it was
essential that we learned to get those inner feelings out of ourselves right there up front for everyone to see, and hear, and
touch. First the clothes, then the easy feelings, then the tough

feelings, the easy-to-tell secrets, then the hard-to-tell secrets, then the entire inner self. And when all this stuff had been exposed and we were just about psychologically everted, the reality of psychological private property would be obliterated and we would be free, or equal, or renewed—or something.

Almost any history of a small town contains references to gossips, informants, distributors of illicit news. These histories reveal both the need of people to have their private news broadcast on gossip circuits, and the need to receive some affirmation of their status by giving or hearing news in return.

In the United States, the advice to the lovelorn column, and most conspiciously, the gossip magazine, gradually turned the expression of private fears and wonderings into a multi-million dollar business. In the fifties, there was an exposé rage. Movie stars, the objects of our erotic and infantile fantasies, became the victims, along with athletes and political figures. If a person did anything public, there was no justifiable reason for that person to claim any right to privacy. The exposé magazines entered the bedrooms of these people; Hefner-like industries undressed them; television and newspapers probed whatever was left. Some of America's stars loved this sensuous trespassing on their private property, some of them fought the exposure hounds. What too many of the trespassers forgot was that even the most narcissistic of us occasionally needs to worship our own reflections in private.

Then too, the 1940s and 1950s ushered in the paranoia about communism, that seemingly fuzzy body of political theory which in fact contained some rather trenchant notions about private ownership and free speech. So, while some dug around in the social lives of celebrities, others dug into files and private papers and eventually into the ideologies, psychologies, philosophies, indeed into the very minds of men and women. What had been covered was exposed; what had been silenced was made audible to the point of its being deafening; what had been discretely private was made outrageously public. At that point almost an entire culture was involved with erasing a significant boundary line between public and private domains, between collective and individual existence.

The issue of whether or not an individual has any right to privacy or even to value privacy was complicated not only by the actions of the media, but also by research findings and the dissemination of these findings. Countries have always spied on one another, as have competing industries. Keeping watch on next-door neighbors is no new business as Thorstein Veblen made clear, and as David Riesman articulated in his description of the other-directed person in *The Lonely Crowd*.* But in the last thirty years, research in the natural and social sciences also has been influenced by the desire to divulge the mysteries of the universe. An ethic of investigative reporting has grown up in the enterprises of many researchers. While some scientists work—as we imagine scientists have always worked—quietly, modestly, amidst their mysterious paraphernalia and idiosyncrasies, other scientists push for divulgence and recognition, seemingly unaffected by the personal hurt such divulgences may cause, or what ramifications might ensue from their hunt for recognition.

In its schools, this country has seen a revolutionary transformation in attitudes. Granted, since the turn of the century public schools enunciated personal development, discipline, and getting along with others as the major purposes of education. In the last decade, however, the classroom has fostered both the colossal rise of a business known as psychology, and the growth of an apparatus known as guidance counseling. In many grammar schools now, one finds compulsory sensitivity or human growth groups where children as young as six years old are obliged to reveal intimate feelings as well as attitudes toward one another. In some of these programs, children earn points for their team merely by talking. Thus, taciturn children run the risk of seeing themselves as "problematic," not to mention losing the game for their team. While the children sit in their little chairs feeling the assault on their little psyches, their parents—in after-school programs, most of which, thankfully, are voluntary—sit in their big chairs feeling the assault on their big psyches.

It all seems bizarre as one describes it, but the preoccupation with people revealing and divulging has gone far beyond what many of us imagined. In California schools, professionals are beginning to diagnose a new childhood illness called shyness, from the Middle English "schei," meaning, alas, timidity. It has been deemed pathological, dangerous for the child. In some cases, drugs are administered to these children in order to "open them up" and have at least some of "it" hang out. In many schools, the value of individual study habits and working alone, encased in one's privacy, has been philosophically and architecturally precluded. Consider a simple

*New Haven: Yale University Press, 1950.

question: On what surface should children write? A desk in which they can store their own belongings, or a table where space, by necessity, is shared with three or four other children? The mere presence of the desk or table bespeaks the value that a particular school places on individual learning or collective learning. While myriad factors obviously go into the decision of desks or tables, open classrooms or closed ones, rooms without walls or spaces with built-in cubbies, one might well discover that schools without desks are also schools with elaborate guidance personnel systems.

The major point one draws from the increased use of mental health facilities in schools is that certain educators believe that affective learning is as important to a child's development as is cognitive learning. Once, there seemed to be a distinct separation of these two approaches. One either advocated traditional pedagogic and traditional course work, or one argued for sensitivity training, psychological openness, and the *feeling* of learning.

The disparity between these two philosophies partly reflected the traditional distinction between the child-rearing role of the family on the one hand, and that of the church and school on the other. Historically, it was the family's responsibility to shape its children's emotional lives. Schools were meant for learning, the church for moral development. Now, with the influx of mental health workers and psychological researchers, schools are taking responsibility for cognitive, emotional, and moral development. In this regard, families have also been pried open and their once-private negotiations made public. Thus one finds traditional structures underwriting affective educational procedures, and in consequence, sensitivity training is valued in the same way as language arts, social studies, and mathematics. One of the more distressing results of this human growth industry in schools and the more general popularization of psychology is that too many people have actually been trained to believe that only professionals can deal with their children.

In the practice of psychotherapy, a similar though frequently inadvertent attack on privacy has been lodged. Medicine and its allied fields of healing have always confronted the question of which patients receive special treatment and which ones can rightly be used as case studies. Once it was the rich, in their private rooms with private records, and as much anonymity as hospitals could muster who were allowed the greatest privacy. Public clinics meant public knowledge of patient, illness, treatment. The poor were used as specimens, displays, for experimentation. In mental health treatment, this same pattern held. The names of wealthier patients—those referred to as private patients—were withheld from practically everyone, while the names of clinic patients were bandied about hospital meetings and social gatherings.

Someone once wrote that studying the poor is called sociology, studying the rich, exposé. This distinction may no longer be valid, for now even the rich cannot be assured of privacy or immunity from being used as specimens for grand rounds. Similarly, one finds a great many psychotherapists revealing facts about their patients to the point where patients' identities can easily be inferred. While confidentiality may be promised by psychotherapists, it frequently is not delivered. One hears stories of videotapes of patients being played for audiences, some of them not even professional therapists, when patients are not aware of this practice. One hears the spouse of a psychotherapist speaking about patients, occasionally even by name. Indeed one hears many patients speaking about their therapists. Apparently these people assume that their own psychotherapy is an act necessarily open for public consumption. Someone recently likened the announcement that one is entering psychoanalysis to the announcement of a birth of a child. "With great pleasure and extreme humility, Thomas J. Cottle is proud to announce the birth of a 190-pound character disorder with underlying depressive traits." Can anyone anymore assume confidentiality? Can anyone guarantee it?

Research subjects, too, are often left unprotected by investigators. Having been promised confidentiality, their names, interview protocols, test results are discussed in the cafeterias, offices, and elevators of research institutions and universities in the same way and with the same irreverence with which one discusses professional athletes. There are always the careful therapists and researchers who abide by the covenants of confidentiality, but transgressors abound. Like adolescents experiencing sexuality for the first time, they must tell all.

If one recalls one's grammar school and high school days, images quickly return of students daring one another to try something, forcing one another to engage in some act. Peer pressure always has been around, but it is now being accentuated by the growing ethic to make the private public. Free speech has been turned on its head. Divulgence and revelation are the battle cries. Nothing human beings do must remain secret; no one is to be reclusive; nothing about the body must be mysterious. As the physiology and biochemistry of the brain are slowly, slowly understood, the contents of one's mind must be quickly, quickly reported. If it takes drugs, electric shock, psychosurgery, or some other form of artificial stimulation to open us up to new experiences, new levels of consciousness, new forms of public display, then we will not only embrace these stimuli, but we will develop astonishing rationales for their value and locate some grand historical moment when people contemplated similar ideals. It's becoming so hard nowadays to keep a secret, so hard to lose one's job or virginity, one's identity or sanity, one's health or loved ones, and not write a book about it. Holding things in is dirty, letting them out is cleansing. There can be no more fright when one's inner world is seen in the light of day, in the presence of other people. When we tell everything no one can control us.

One of the sad ironies of America's mania to expose everything and make privacy an impossible reality, is that those who present themselves as anticapitalists have in fact found a new commodity, the inner life, which becomes a marvelous source of profit. About the only book not yet written in that how-to-live-your-life category is how to survive in the face of the onslaught of how-to-live-your-life books. The sequel to Eric Berne's volume, *What to Say After You Say Hello*, might well be, *I'm Leaving Now; Hello Is All I Wanted to Say*. The new profit takers of revelation may be fighting the old warhorses of individualism, existential aloneness, and what David Bakan called the agentic quality of human endeavor.* Their hopes, presumably, are to replace these old spirits with a public effort at communalism, the sharing of all goods and services, and a society based on the collectivization of everything from family to industry to government to people's unconsciousness.

The danger lies, as it always has, in coercing people to reveal that which they prefer to hide. The problem, as educators and physicians well know, is how to keep everyone's records private when the police, employers, armed forces, and insurance companies insist on inspecting these records. The danger is that with an enormous amount of information being col-

*The Duality of Human Existence. Chicago: Rand McNally, 1966.

lected by hundreds of agencies on millions of people, there will come a movement to predict human behavior instead of just analyse it—which often seems bad enough—and to control behavior on the basis of what *might* evolve. Without valuing private behavior and in opening all records, we will begin to treat people as *potential* psychopaths, *potential* criminals, *potential* delinquents, *potential* assassins. In fact this movement has already begun. We are less than a decade away from 1984. The danger is that the FBI and CIA will continue to spy on citizens, and that reputable newspapers, themselves decrying yellow journalism, will print the findings that the CIA and FBI uncovered but had never before made public. Already there have been victims of this so-called legitimate revelatory reportage.

The purpose of any sane political ideology should be freedom for all human beings. In psychological terms, we want all people to experience the feeling of freedom and be affirmed in their desire to feel free. In many instances, divulgence, revelation, candor, yield a wondrous sensation of being free. Unquestionably, people must be able to free themselves of ideas and emotions which trouble them and upset their relationships with others, and which in many cases confuse and damage institutions. Children must be allowed to safely reveal their problems to school personnel, workers their inner worlds to one another and their employers, family members to one another. The quest for knowledge must never cease. One might even say, albeit reluctantly, that people have a need to confess or let others know bits and pieces of their private selves.

But if there is a need to reveal, there is also a need to protect and withhold. We may be making a grievous mistake in forcing people to believe that every secret, every sentiment, every inner inch of themselves must be exposed. Freedom of speech must not be confused with perpetual human openness. One is not attacking the concept of private ownership or safeguarding the First Amendment by supporting publicness at all costs. One is merely creating another artificial need, the need to cleanse by candor and exposure. Watergate administrations, foul dealings in industry, CIA interventions in foreign countries, the oppression of peoples, these must be exposed and expunged. But as the oppressed of the world well know, freedom demands restraints. How many thousands of times one hears in conversations with the poor of this land, "The government can make all the rules for living, but it will never tell me what to think, what to say, and when to say it."

Sometimes the poor reveal a quality and intensity of expressiveness and openness unmatched in our society. Their openness and seeming lack of privacy is so dazzling, one believes they have never known constraint. At other times, however, they reveal that posture, that way of surviving in the world they first called, and now we call, "cool." Suddenly the expressiveness and openness vanish, and we have no idea what plays in their heads. We have no sense of their attitudes toward us, no idea of their plans. The cool ones, like the silent and reclusive ones, frighten us. It is best to know where they stand, what they think, what they feel. When they reveal themselves, we have some hold on them.

The balance between personal and societal exposure on the one hand, and privacy on the other, is precarious, to say the least. Presently, a band of new profiteers is yanking us toward a world without personal protection, fences, shower curtains, clothes, a world of eternal lightness, without shadows, without night. Some of us prefer to hold on to a few secrets. We don't fear psychoanalysis stripping us of our meager bursts of creativity; we fear the ethic of publicness ripping away those private vessels in which the fluid of life is kept fresh, if not always pure. We fear a point in time when, after accommodating ourselves to seeing nakedness on television, and then sexual behavior on television, and then sexual behavior in the midst of family therapy sessions on television, and then videotape feedbacks of ourselves watching sexual behavior among and between several species in the midst of interphylogenetic therapy sessions on television, the tube will suddenly glow white, and all the lights of our homes will glow light, and the light outside will blaze, and we will see nothing and feel nothing.

Part Two

Observations
of Children
and
Young People

It is hard to believe that ten years have passed since I first began speaking with families in the Boston area. The children I know have grown so much. Some of them, who weren't even old enough to speak with me when I first visited their homes, now are thinking about high school.

One such person is thirteen-year-old Delores Patterson, whose classmates call her Del or the Big D. She was tall when she was five years old, I remember, on the thin side, quiet, but certainly not lacking in energy. Her parents watched her development closely, perhaps a bit too closely, I used to think leaving the Patterson home in a working-class district of Massachusetts. Perhaps they were hoping to hold on to Delores since she was the only girl in the family, the last child at that. Still, their concern with her capacities seemed excessive.

In time, their concern came to be shared with many people, for Delores, as her parents knew when she was very small, was afflicted with some form of dystrophy, a mysterious and evil disease that would slowly but inevitably cut into her muscles until finally she would be without the use of her legs, and possibly later on, her arms as well. So Barbara and Ted Patterson's attention to their only daughter was not excessive at all. They were merely watching for the signs of the illness that grew in their child's body and would soon transform her from what we often unthinkingly call a normal child, to what we unthinkingly call a handicapped child.

Delores Patterson, thirteen, an eighth-grade student in a junior high school, always smiles when we meet. Her look is one of pleasure and surprise with just a trace of good-natured irritation. It's as if she where asking, why would you come back to speak to me again? There's nothing in my life that could possibly interest anyone. In fact, she has said these very words. I remember, for example, a conversation on a lovely May afternoon. Delores wore jeans and a bright red sweatshirt with the words "New England Patriots" written across the front of it. Her long black hair shone in the daylight as it fell down behind the green leather back of her wheel chair. She had asked me to push her along a path in a park near her home. To reach the particular area of the park she liked so well meant lifting her up several stairs. She enjoyed my efforts and swearing at the cumbersome wheel chair. The excursion was to be somewhat of a test for me, she said with a grin, but I knew when I turned away from her and concentrated on my task, that a feeling of sadness and embarrassment came over her. She spoke about the matter of embarrassment that afternoon.

"I like school," she began. "Sometimes I feel I like it too much, more than the other kids in my class. Maybe it's 'cause I feel that all I *can* do is school. When they're outside running around, I have to be here. I can't go any place. It's just as easy to be reading or doing my work. So it turns out that I start doing better in school than some of them. It's not that I'm smarter. I know that's not true 'cause I can hear how smart they are when they talk in class. It's only that I work harder, I have more time. They do many other things and I can only do a few. So it's only right that I'm a little bit better than them. That's just another thing that makes me feel embarrassed too."

"Another thing?" I wondered.

"I do have my days when I'm embarrassed about being like this. Nobody says things to me, but I hear some of the kids joking every once in a while. 'Look out, here comes Ironside,' they'll say. Or, one of the boys is always talking about me pulling into a filling station for gas and oil. Lots of times I'm embarrassed just being the person I am. Then, like, maybe I'll do real well in class, maybe even get the highest grade of anybody, and all the kids tell me how wonderful it is, and how glad they are that I got the highest grade, and that's just embarrassing all over again. See what I mean? Either they're feeling sorry for me or making fun of me, in a good way I mean, or rooting real hard for me to do well." Delores pounded the arm rest of the wheel chair and looked straight ahead. "When you have this tagging along with you, there's no way people treat you like you were normal. *I* know I'm not normal. Anyone who's seen as many doctors as I have knows they're not normal. My God, the first ten years of my life, I'll bet I spent more time in doctors' offices than all the kids in my class combined. And multiplied by ten!"

"They've really examined you top to bottom, haven't they, D?"

"Everywhere. I'm like a walking experiment." Delores heard the words as I had. She looked at me, not smiling this time, but with an expression that could only be read as, pretty pathetic, eh? "I talked to a little boy a few days ago," she continued. "He was telling his teacher that no matter what anybody said and no matter how hard everybody tried, he couldn't learn to spell. He either couldn't see the words in his head or didn't like the alphabet. I don't know which. I happened to be there 'cause I work with the little kids once in a while, usually while my class is at gym. So I told him, 'Roland, you can learn to do anything you want. Some things are hard to do and some things are easy. Most of us don't like to do the hard ones 'cause we do the easy things so well. But you got to learn how to spell. You will if you just start working at it like your teacher's trying to tell you.' He has a great teacher. Miss Michaelson. I had her too. So what does little Roland say? He looks at me like I'm some sort of monster, which I suppose I am for him, for other people too, and he says, 'Can you learn to walk if you want to?' I mean, I was shocked. I didn't know what to say."

"Did he really want an answer?"

"He did. He really did. I didn't say anything, thinking he'd start talking about something else, but he wanted an answer. So I said to him, 'I will never learn how to walk. It's not that I don't want to, I just can't. All the wanting in the world won't let me walk.' So he said, 'And all the wanting in the world won't let me spell,' and he started to walk away. Miss Michaelson was there. I could tell she was ready to give up on him. But I called him back. 'Roland,' I told him, 'you think I can't learn to walk, right? And you think you can't learn to spell, right? And you think they're the same, right?' You should have seen him nodding his head. Then I said, 'But here's where you're wrong. Once upon a time I *could* walk. I *did* walk. But once upon a time you *never* could spell. So you have to learn. When you do, you have the right to forget it, like I have the right not to walk again.' "

"What'd he say to that?"

"Nothing. He seemed to be interested in what I was telling him. Miss Michaelson took him away as fast as she could. She thanked me for trying. I could tell she was starting to cry. That's one of the times when I'm embarrassed about all this." Delores's left hand fell in her lap. With her right hand she made a fist, and now as we sat silently glancing about the small park, I heard her thumping the arm of the wheel chair.

Ted Patterson had wasted no time negotiating with schools when he realized his daughter would need special facilities. One of the neighborhood public schools turned him down flatly when he requested aid. Another school said it wanted to help but didn't have the technology. A third indicated there was no problem in Delores attending the school if someone could figure out how she would navigate the stairs. Still, the

Pattersons persisted, exploring schools, interviewing teachers, administrators, men and women involved in special education programs. At last a school accepted Delores and even urged her parents to participate in the special teaching their daughter required.

"We were lucky," Delores told me that day in the park when I reminded her of the difficulty of finding a school. "We were really lucky. No matter what anybody says, a handicapped child is a pain in the neck for anybody who spends time with them, especially teachers. Even you, Cottle," she pointed her finger at my nose. " 'Member how you were groaning lifting me up those stairs?"

"I was only teasing," I protested with embarrassment.

"I know, but it's a sign that I'm a bit of a burden. Maybe not a whole burden but part of one. How about when you lifted me out of the car before? You couldn't have liked that. I know people are always doing things for me and that I'm not supposed to feel sorry for myself. All the TV shows on handicapped people, that's all they ever say, don't feel sorry for yourself. But still we were lucky with this school. I know kids from the hospitals who are blind and deaf who've never even been in school. Maybe they started out but then they stopped 'cause they couldn't get special help. God, I don't know how you could go to school and not see. And if you couldn't hear," she shuddered, "it'd be awful. I'm lucky 'cause all I need is ramps or elevators or somebody to lift me up once in a while. I can make it."

"Were there special schools you could have gone to?"

" I suppose so, but I don't see myself as, like, sick, like I belong in a *whole* special school. There's nothing wrong with my brain. You know what?" she interrupted herself. "When I was about, maybe seven, this woman my mother talked to wanted to put me in a school for handicapped kids. I guess my mother was real excited 'cause they couldn't find any other place for me. So they took me out to this school in the country which turned out to be part of a mental hospital. The school was for brain-damaged children, like retarded children, you know. People still think if you have one handicap you have them all.

"Sometimes when I talk with people in my school, even some of the teachers, I can tell they're trying not to mention my being in a wheel chair, which I can understand. But then I imagine they're looking at me like they're trying to find out whether I'm also blind or deaf, or whether something's wrong with my brain. Once I saw this assistant principal looking at me really funny. So I said to him, 'There's nothing wrong with my brain. I'm not retarded.' He said he wasn't thinking that at all. He was thinking about his own baby who was just born, like two days before, and the baby was in one of those special things, you know . . .''

"An incubator?"

"Yes, and he was worried because he had just read a story about how some baby in an incubator hadn't gotten enough air to breathe and went blind. He asked me if I knew anything about that. He was really upset. I wanted to help him. I told him I was never in that part of the hospital when I was sick. I don't think he heard me."

Whenever I ask Delores about her plans for some event, even one as small as an upcoming project for school, it becomes an occasion for her to tell me how she sees time unravelling in her life. It is in these moments that I feel her working to transcend the past and put aside thoughts of what the future might bring. In all of our conversations this issue of not letting time oppress her rises to the surface. In the park that one afternoon it took this form:

"The problem at school is that I don't want people to think of me only as the handicapped girl, the kid in the wheel chair. I want them to think of me as a person too, a whole person. I know that sounds corny. Everybody says that. But I guess I'm not really a whole person, to *them*, I mean. To *me* I am. I don't think about what I am and the problems I have which most people don't have, but I *am* a whole person. They try at school, I suppose, but it's hard for them. Then sometimes, like when I need help, it's like I'm reminding them that I'm not really a whole person 'cause I can't get out of this." I watched her grip the arms of the chair. "So really what I'm saying is that I want them to see me as a whole person even though I know and they know there are times I need help. It *is* like that little boy Roland who thought he couldn't spell. It didn't mean he wasn't a complete whole person though.

"Maybe I was once. Maybe when I could walk and run I didn't think about anything being in the past or future. Now I feel I have to hurry and do things. It's like I can worry about the past but I have to, like, race the future. What's going to get me first, my illness or my learning everything in school? Nobody can ever know how I feel when there's something that the school keeps from me because I'm in a wheel chair. I always want to say, give me everything you can, don't hold back, I don't know how much time I have. And remember all the kids who want to go to school who have handicaps and can't get in anywhere. I was lucky. You can fool yourself by saying things could be worse. My father always tells me that. 'Things could be worse, Delores.' Maybe he's right. Can you imagine if I was like this, maybe not even as bad, and I didn't have school?" Delores looked about, her gestures causing me to take in the scene of children playing, running, climbing on jungle gyms, working intently in the large sandbox. "I can't run with these children," I heard her say, "but I can use my brain as well as they'll ever be able to. Nobody can change that. I have school, my studies . . ."

"Your friends . . ."

"My friends."

During the years I have known of Delores's illness and confinement in the wheel chair, I have been aware of some of the problems she has experienced with friends. Many of the children, especially when she was very young, were confused by her illness and chose to ignore her entirely, or pretended they didn't see anything wrong with her. Others laughed openly, or kept quiet their jokes and grotesque impersonations of her until she was out of hearing and seeing distance. These children, however, rarely broke her spirit. Her parents and several teachers warned her of this part of school life.

As she grew older, what hurt her more was seeing the natural constraints being placed on close friendships. Perhaps it was a group of girls talking together with Delores after class. The conversation would grow in excitement and somebody would suggest that they run downstairs and continue the conversation outside on the school steps. Suddenly they'd be gone, and in their enthusiasm and camaraderie they'd have forgotten Delores and the difficulties she faced navigating stairs. Or maybe it would be a bunch of boys and girls strolling together after school near the very park where Delores and I were now sitting. Gradually people would be pairing off, moving here and there, not far from her, but unaware that there may be areas of intimacy from which she was excluded. When I asked her once about these moments, she seemed, naturally, reluctant to respond.

"I always carry a book with me. Be prepared," she said with a faint smile. "They don't mean it. You get caught up in your own thoughts and you forget sometimes. My God, I forget my parent's birthdays sometimes. Besides, how many times have I gone off talking in class or helping someone with homework and they don't even know what I'm talking about. I'm so interested in *my* interests, I don't stop and think about the other person and what they might be interested in. I think all of us are thoughtless like that once in a while. I don't blame anyone for forgetting me and my stupid ugly wheel chair."

One draws strength talking with people like the young woman I now was pushing through the little park. It is trite, sentimental, this feeling, but it is true, and very real. This child makes me feel strong and ashamed about many things, hopeful and sad at the same time. She seems older than I, and yet younger too, and she recognizes the moods and feelings she evokes in me and in the other people she befriends. She knows when her parents are trying to hide their bitterness about her condition, or when a teacher is frustrated by something she has done or, more likely, is unable to do. On some occasions, Delores has even told a teacher, "Go ahead, say what you're thinking. *I* hate this wheel chair more than you do."

She knows too what the children her age think and feel about her. She sees the expression in the eyes of the little ones like Roland, whose searching look of wonderment practically screams out the words, "Why can't you stand up and be like the rest of us?" She knows the shame that follows the inadvertent thoughtlessness of her friends. She told me once how three boys, all good friends of hers, accidentally forgot to pick her up after school and left her sitting on a stoop with her wheel chair fifteen feet away. It was an hour before someone came and took her home.

We had reached my car and I began making preparations to lift Delores into the front seat. A man nearby offered to help. Listening carefully to Delores's instructions for the move, we reached down and in an instant had her comfortably placed in the car.

"You two guys are really good at this," she said, nodding to each of us. "Don't forget my wheels, Cottle," she reminded me. "Maybe I ought to take you with me wherever I go. You could be like my private bodyguards." She made an exaggerated groaning noise. "That was a bad joke."

"I didn't even get it," I mumbled.

"Bodyguards? Bodyguards?"

"Then I was driving toward her home. On the way, she

made me go past the local high school where she would be enrolling soon.

"That's the big goal, right there," she said with excitement. "That's what I'm pushing for. Then college. That's the single thing I think about. I don't even know whether there are ramps in that building. I'm afraid to find out. My luck, I won't be able to go there. But I'll find some place, even if I have to go to Hawaii."

"Now *that* wouldn't be bad."

"It would be good, they don't have winters there. I hate winters 'cause of that thing." She looked toward the back seat where I had stored the wheel chair. "Mrs. Thurmond, my sixth grade teacher, promised me I'd get into high school."

"What's your worry?" I asked unthinkingly. "With *your* grades?"

"Grades aren't the only thing, Cottle. Don't forget, I'm one of those special student types. I don't just automatically pass from one grade to the next, and especially one building to the next. Everything has to be checked out, all those little things people like you take for granted. Like, is there a girls' lavatory that doesn't have sixty million stairs to climb. We're a problem, we special students, haven't you heard? Even if we're in the top three percent of our class, we're a problem. Nobody likes special students if special means different."

For several minutes Delores and I drove on in silence. She looked out at the neighborhood she knew so well as if she were seeing it for the first time. Everything, it seemed, caught her attention.

"I think you're going to make it," I said at last. "Fact is, I don't have the slightest doubt."

"I do too, Cottle," she answered smartly. "Fact, I know I will, if enough people in the school give me the chance."

I turned right on Medford Street. The Patterson home was in the middle of the block. "They will, " I said.

"We'll see," she replied softly. "We'll see."

T he few people who have known Angela Margaretti all her life agree that she has the same face now that she had when she was but a few months old. The same enormous brown eyes, the same high cheek bones, the long lashes, the perfectly shaped ears. It's the same face, they say, the same baby face. It's like Angela's body continued to age and mature but her face stayed the same. Her relatives always looked at her in envy, for not only at twelve years of age was she growing up to be a beautiful woman, she would be one of those lucky people who look years younger than they really are. A child to be envied, her relatives always said. Even if the Margaretti family was on welfare and Angela's father Dante had disappeared a month before his daughter's fourth birthday, even if the school she attended was run-down, even if she had to do without so many of the things that children her age took for granted, she was a child to be envied.

I came to know the Margaretti family when Mrs. Anna Margaretti, Angela's mother, was just recovering from an accident —a boy on a bicycle had sped around a corner and hit her head-on, knocking her into a traffic light. We began conversing at the hospital, and when she left, I promised I would visit her at home as well. A pleasant woman who seemed to vacillate between periods of wanting to talk and periods when she barely spoke with anyone, Anna Margaretti never told me anything about the way she was leading her life or had led her life for the past ten years. All I knew was that she worked somewhere in the evenings, slept late in the mornings, and usually was away from the house in the afternoons when her daughter arrived home from school. Her own parents were dead, but residing in the neighborhood near her were several cousins and some old childhood friends who claimed they might just as well have been related to her.

With her mother away so often, it was only natural that Angela Margaretti learned the value of self-sufficiency early. She was used to going to sleep in an empty apartment, fixing dinner and breakfast for herself, and cleaning the two and a half rooms she shared with her mother. She was also reconciled to the fact that there was rarely food in the house and never enough money to buy clothes and other things she might have wanted. But as she always told me, "You get used to all this. It doesn't make me special. I don't want people to feel sorry for me. When I was five and six years old, I was living my life just like I'm living it right now. My body's getting old but all the things around me are staying pretty much the way they've always been. My cousins and aunts always tell me my face and my expressions haven't changed since I was a baby. I can't believe that. But I do know that my life hasn't changed that much. It surely didn't change when Mom took her jobs in the evening. I was on my own before then. It didn't even change that much when my father went away. I was four, so I wasn't doing my own cooking, of course, but they always left me alone. I remember coming in from playing, you know, like at dinner time, and there wouldn't be anyone here. They were out some place together, probably apart more likely. So I just had to manage. There really wasn't that much to it. Lots of kids do it. You may not like everything you have to do, but if you have to do it, you do it. Simple, right?"

If I was made uncomfortable in the Margaretti apartment by the poverty, by the loneliness that I saw in both of these people, and by the chaotic quality that dominated their lives, I was made even more uncomfortable by a secret, a terribly important secret that I felt they were keeping not only from me, but from everybody. In some families one senses that while out of discretion many personal issues are not discussed with friends, a fundamental honesty and openness characterize the family. In other families—and the Margarettis clearly belonged to this second group—while a great many personal issues are divulged as friendships become closer and more significant, a whole body of information never seems to reach the surface. In these cases one presumes that the family has made a pact not to disclose certain information. So while the people themselves are not exactly suspicious, one cannot help but suspect something when speaking with them. Furthermore, in many homes in poor and working-class communities, where money is tight, prospects for work bleaker than they have ever been, and where prices for everything go higher and higher each day, one suspects that someone in a family may be in trouble. Maybe there's a psychological problem, maybe someone's been drinking, maybe someone's in debt to the point that his or her life is being threatened, maybe someone is running with a bad crowd, being led into the rackets.

On a bright April day, Angela Margaretti called me to say that her mother had been picked up by the police.

"What's the charge?" I asked.

" I don't know." Angela was crying. "Someone said some-

thing about a woman being killed. Maybe drugs. Can you
come over?"

When I got to the Margaretti's apartment Angela was not there. She left a note saying she had gone to the jail where they were keeping her mother and that she would return. I waited a long while, then decided to leave. As I drove off I saw Angela running down the street, obviously hurrying to catch me. Although it was chilly that day for April, she wore only a blouse, a skirt, and sandals. Her look was one of desperation.

"It's drugs," she whispered, out of breath from having run all the way from the precinct office where her mother had been booked. "She's involved in selling drugs. I don't know the whole story. Something about someone who got angry at this guy my mother's been seeing and told the police. He's supposed to get off because he confessed. I don't know." Angela was shivering and perspiring at the same time. "I'm going to have a mother in prison," she wept as I led her up the apartment house stairs. "What will happen? What will happen? I'm going to be without a mother and a father, and I'm a baby. I'm a child. That's all I am. Everyone thinks I'm strong 'cause I don't need them, 'cause I cook and take care of everything. But I'm a baby. I'm just like a newborn baby except now I don't have any parents. I don't have anybody."

There was no way I could stop Angela from crying. The Margarettis had no phone and the Blyles who lived next door on the same floor were out. Their front door was open and a putrid odor of rotten food came from the kitchen. The Margaretti's small refrigerator was not only empty of milk or fruit or anything else I could offer to Angela, the motor had stopped. In fact there was no electricity anywhere in the apartment. The kitchen clock had stopped about the time Angela had called me, probably from Stephano's, the hot dog and pizza place around the corner. In the space that served as the living room, dining room, and Angela's bedroom—Anna used the room on the other side of the kitchen for her bedroom—I tried to comfort a twelve-year-old girl who was firmly convinced that she would never see her mother again and that she would not survive.

"I'm a baby," she repeated over and over again. "Can't they let my mother out because she has to take care of me? You could tell them I'm a baby, they'd never have to find out.

They'd believe *you*. You could tell them I'm sick, like a crip-
ple. Tell them I can't be left alone. Someone has to feed me.
They know we don't have a lot of money. All they have to
do is come here and they can see that. We could rent a wheel
chair and when they come I'll sit in it with a blanket on me.
Tell them. Tell them I can't be alone. I've never been alone.
Who's going to live with me and take care of me? It isn't fair
that they put her in jail if she's a mother. Mothers can't go to
jail. They're supposed to take care of their children. I don't
even have brothers and sisters. I'm alone. They can see that.
You can tell them. Like, no one's ever here in this apartment
building, right? So if there's a fire or something I could die,
and because they had my mother in jail they'd be responsible,
right? Wouldn't they be responsible? It's not my fault there
weren't grownups here. They're the ones who took her away.
Mother!" She screamed out loudly. "*Mother!* What are we
going to do? How am I going to live? I don't even know if I
can see her. She could be a million miles from here for all I
know. Oh God. I don't even know where my own mother
is. She could be out of the country. *Mother!* Is she in her
room?" Angela looked in the direction of her mother's bedroom. "Nobody's told me what she's done. How do they know
what she's done. The men did it. I'm sure the men did. Arnie.
That guy Arnie. Anything she did he made her do. Why don't
they find out about *that*? It doesn't matter with him. He
doesn't have a family. But my mother has one. You can't take
a mother away from a child. If you take a mother away from
her child, her child dies. Let them take Arnie and all his ugly
friends. They made her do it. *Mother!*" she called out again.
"You're going to have to do something." Angela looked at
me. Her face was wet with tears and she kept pushing back her
hair with the heels of her hand. "You have to get her out. And
if you can't, then you got to get me in there to see her. I'm
not staying here alone. I'm getting out of here the second you
leave. I'm not staying. I want to be where she is. I'm really
not staying. You think I am 'cause I stayed here all those
nights when she was out working. But that was different. I'm
not staying any more. At least then I knew when she was
coming back. But I'm not staying alone. I'm a *baby*. They
have to take care of me. If they can't, they have to let my
mother out. *Mother!*"

   In the following weeks the legal case against Anna Margaretti became clear. She and two other men had been involved

with the import and sale of cocaine and heroin. Although Anna
was only implicated in the case, in the end she was sentenced
to several years in jail. Apparently she had been present when
one of her two men friends sold drugs to an undercover nar-
cotics agent. While her friends and members of her family
claimed she had received little or no legal defense, the case
against her was so strong that there was probably little any
lawyer could have done to prevent her from going to jail.

Angela went to her mother's trial but found the ordeal too
painful. After sitting in the court for the first day's session,
she decided not to return. She waited in the large hall outside the courtroom the morning her mother was sentenced.
By the time she learned what had happened, her mother had
already been led out of the courtroom through a side door.
The mother and daughter did not see each other until later
that night at the jail. The next day Anna was taken to the institution where she would remain for a minimum of two years.

In the first six months of her mother's imprisonment, Angela Margaretti lived in the home of a cousin. The Passows insisted that she come home with them. The location of their
apartment was ideal, they said, only blocks from Angela's
school. Everyone thought it was a good idea. After six months,
however, Angela sought housing elsewhere. The Passows, she
claimed, were too cruel to one another and to their own children, although never to her. In fact the lack of fairness they
demonstrated to their children was one of Angela's major reasons for wanting to leave. The Passows insisted that she remain
with them, but she told them she couldn't stand being with
them any longer.

At the end of the school year Angela moved into the home
of another family, the Perinis who, while they were not related to the Margarettis, seemed as close as family. The atmos-
phere in this home was more pleasant, although Cesar Perini
made constant references to Anna's trial and prison sentence.
He demanded to know what Angela spoke about with her
mother on her visits to the prison, something which made
Angela feel uncomfortable. Fortunately, Maria Perini, a woman in her late forties who had worked for years as a hospital
technician, remonstrated with her husband, reminding him
again and again that what went on between Angela and her
mother was nobody's business.

Indeed what transpired in the conversations between Angela and her mother was known to no one. My own visits with

Angela continued almost weekly for the entire period of her mother's imprisonment. I often drove her to the prison, waited for her to come out, and drove her back to the Perini's. Not until a month before her mother's release did she ever reveal her feelings about her mother's circumstances. Usually she would descend the front stairs of the prison, enter my car, and begin to speak about something we both knew was insignificant.

"This is the middle of October," she would say to me, "isn't it?"

"Seventeenth today," I'd say.

"Isn't it time for the World Series to start?"

"It's all over. Oakland won."

"Oh, that's right. I heard them talking about it on television." Her eyes would be wet with tears. Then we would drive on, usually in silence, occasionally speaking about school, the Perinis, a boy friend.

On one of her last visits to the prison before her mother's release, fourteen-year-old Angela Margaretti spoke briefly about what she had been carrying in her heart over the last two years. After thanking me for the rides to the prison, she insisted that she wanted to pick up her mother without me. For the final trip she preferred to take the bus. It had to be a day for the two of them to be alone, she said.

"I don't know whether I've been dreaming of this day. Maybe I have. I don't think anybody thinks about any one thing *all* of the time. But I sure am glad it's over. I didn't think the time would ever pass. I'm proud of my mother. She's changed in these two years, you know. I guess she's learned her lesson. Some people in my school heard something about her. They didn't know what had happened. In the beginning I told some of the kids my mother died. Then later I changed my story. I told them she went away. 'I thought you said she died,' they said. 'I never said that.' 'Yes, you did,' they said. I was ashamed of her then. I hated her for being in prison. I hated me and everybody. I even started hating my father all over again and I sure thought I was done with him, in my mind I mean.

"Sometimes you don't know what to feel about a mother like the one I have. First you hate her, then you love her. Then you tell yourself you have to decide which one it is. It's not easy, you know. I was ashamed to be her daughter. Some kids say their mother does this or that but I have to say my moth-

er's a convict. I couldn't even use the excuse that she was in-
nocent 'cause she told me she wasn't. She admitted everything
they said she did. I think that was good for her to do. But like,
I had no mother for two years. You have to think about *my*
side of the picture too. I've never really had a father and now
for two years I didn't have a mother, either. So you have to
think about *me*. But you have to think about *her* too. She had
a lousy time of it. She got mixed up with a lot of bad guys.
That was partly her fault. We spoke a lot about that. She was
lonely. I didn't think much about it when I was young but she
really was by herself. She's an attractive woman too. So she
needed to have men around. Some of them were good, I guess,
and some of them were like those guys she got caught with.
She's not a bad person. If you knew her like I do, you'd know
she wasn't a bad person. She doesn't feel good about this.

"I don't want this to sound like everything's wonderful
again though. It was never wonderful with her, and I can't imagine that it will be wonderful with her now. I'm sure it will
be a lot like it was. She's not going to stay home. But I'm a
lot older now, or at least I feel I am. It's only been two years.
We'll be together and see how it goes. If it works out, fine. If
it doesn't, we'll split up. We decided that. I'll go back with
Maria and her nosy husband and Mom will have to make it
alone. Maybe someday we'll be having our regular weekly
meetings at a restaurant somewhere. Or a bar more likely. Or
maybe she'll end up back in jail. Or maybe *I'll* end up in jail.
If she ends up in there again though I'm not going to visit her.
I've done my time with her. I'll pull a Dante Margaretti on
her and split for good. Then she can go to hell for all I care.
Once in prison is enough. It's once too many for that matter!
I don't have to suffer any more. Nobody's going to make me
suffer any more.

"You know what? I've been listening to me here now the
same way you listen to me and I can't believe I'm still so angry at everything that's happened. 'Member that day they
caught her and I was crying and screaming? I still feel those
feelings inside me, like they never went away. Even though
she went away, those feelings never did. Would have been better if they had gone away with her. I'm proud of my mother
but there's been lots of times I wanted to kill her. That's what
was troubling me all the time when the kids in school asked
me about her. I wanted to be proud of her but I also wanted
to kill her for doing what she did since what she did made me

have to lie about her. So I got angry at the kids when I was really angry at *her*. Then I'd make up my mind to tell her these things and she'd start telling me how lousy my grandmother and grandfather were to her, and all the bad things that Dante did to her when they first got married, so I never said anything. She's had it tough too.

"I'll be gentle with her. I'll be the best I can. I've promised myself that. But if she messes up with me I'm getting out. No more feeling proud when there's no reason for it. And no more hoping she'll be good. If she isn't good now then it's too late. I'll be gone for good, which would be hard I know, 'cause I'm sure way down inside I love her a lot, you know. She is my mother. In the prison or out of it, she's my mother. You can love someone and hate someone at the same time, if they give you reason to love them and hate them. And she does. She isn't the easiest person in the world.

"Okay, so next time, I'll pick her up and take the bus. I want it just the two of us. She can have all the boy friends she wants, but if she messes up this time, then she can just do it all by her little self. I'm not young anymore. When your mother goes to prison, you get real old real quick. Believe me you do. I'm not saying I'm smarter than anyone else, or that I got any smarter just because she's been away. But I'm older than anybody in my school. I'll tell you that for sure. I'm the oldest person there!"

In almost the exact middle of Cauley Street in Brixton, on the top floor of a tan brick row house, is a four-room flat that runs from the front of the building to the rear. The front windows overlook the street, the rear windows overlook the British Railway tracks. The flat is quiet from one in the morning until six. For the remaining hours, the racket on Cauley Street can make you believe you are living in the middle of a football stadium. The noises of people laughing, yelling, bartering, arguing, screaming for their children, or merely passing the time of day is so intense, a person must forfeit any hope of hearing his or her inner voice. The world assaults you in this third-floor flat on Cauley Street, and if you somehow could block out the exterior sounds, the noise coming from the family of eight within the flat would more than make up for that exterior calm.

Frank and Miriam Delano were married in the West Indies and moved to London ten years ago. At the time they had four children. Three more children were born in England but one died from a lung illness before he left the hospital. When Frank Delano lost his job with the West Indian Postal Service, he went to live in the United States. In Connecticut he worked for a tobacco company, in New Jersey for a trucking firm, lifting crates on and off the giant trailers. He was never allowed to drive. When the New Jersey job fell through, for reasons that were never explained to him, he returned to the Islands and managed to find part-time work hauling stone for the terraces being built with the new hotels. But after a year, there was no work.

With money that Miriam's mother had saved from years of working as a chambermaid, the Delanos moved to London, more precisely to Brixton. They preferred to live elsewhere, but an information clerk at Waterloo Station where they first arrived with their four children advised them right off, and with disdain, that "their type" lived either in the district near Nottinghill Gate, or in Brixton. Studying the city's tube plan, they saw it was easier to get from Waterloo Station to Brixton than to Nottinghill Gate, and that's where they went. After ten years in the British capital, they have never visited Nottinghill Gate.

Employment opportunities in England were not as great as the Delanos had been led to believe when in the Islands. There were some jobs, however, and Frank took as many as he could, often working four jobs simultaneously. Miriam found a flat with three bedrooms on Kilmore Street and prospects loomed rather promising. They were disturbed by the London rain and cold, and particularly by the condition of the older children's school, which seemed run-down and uninspiring, but one could not complain. Millions of people in the world, they assured each other, had it far worse than they.

In time, the employment situation worsened. Soon there were only two jobs for Frank, then one, then periods of unemployment, some lasting as long as six months. And there were two more children. With money tight, and England undergoing massive economic inflation, they had no choice but to move to a flat on Cauley Street which was almost as large as the Kilmore Street flat but almost half the cost. It was noisier too, and dirtier and more depressing. Fortunately the children could remain in the same school, but it too had continued to decline in quality, and it never had much of a reputation. Teachers were constantly leaving, and were replaced by others who were inexperienced and intolerant. The Delanos watched innumerable television documentary films and news clips on American slums, and they remarked not on the untenable conditions of America's cities, but on the untenable conditions on Cauley Street. And they listened to London politicians speaking of a race problem that England expected would surface in the next ten years.

Frank Delano is a short, powerfully built man who looks much younger than his forty-six years. He has a full head of hair and such a heavy beard that he often shaves twice a day. He values his clean appearance—clothes pressed, shoes shined, fresh handkerchief—but says his patience, which he had always believed to be his finest quality as it had been his mother's, has long since disappeared. He says too that his spirit is destroyed. If there had been any hope, any optimism about the move to England, it was broken last summer when his son Michael, who everyone calls Mikko, became one of London's many school-leavers. Advised by his teachers to quit school at the age of fifteen, Mikko eagerly set about to find employment. Offices in Brixton and in central London furnished him with lists of potential employers, but nothing materialized. Indeed, Mikko never even felt he had come close to landing a job. So with his teachers seemingly relieved to be rid of him, and his chances for employment next to nothing, he roamed London with a group of boys who spent more time playing the machines in penny arcades than anything else, until one of them, Eddie Balassi, a bloke everyone said slept in his dark brown leather coat, was arrested for breaking into a cleaning shop.

News of Eddie Balassi's arrest almost killed Frank Delano. He did not wish to accept that this was what he would find on emigrating to England. He blamed the country and the government; he spoke of the documentaries he had seen on television; but mostly he blamed the schools.

"Look about this flat," he told me, one bitter cold December afternoon, three weeks after the arrest. The noises rising up from the street were punctuated only by the rush of the trains from the rear of the building, and the room was filled with the odor of Frank Delano's aftershave cologne. "You couldn't live here," he said. "You couldn't bear to live here. Many people would have left long ago. I know that. I know that. But a person can endure it here. You wear every bit of clothing you own in the cold, and rot in the summer from the heat and the smells, but you can endure it. But let them tell me how they keep their schools so bad while the rest of London education is so superior. And I know that to be the case. I know it. I've seen those other communities. I've worked in them for ten years. But look what they provide for us. They keep us away from them, arm's length, letting my children go to school as though they were doing us a favor. They *have* to let my children go to school, and they know it, so they make the schools rotten. I know that they do. They work on it when they can. All they want is to keep the children alive until they are old enough to speak to them about leaving. You know about our famous school-leavers? How they tell children they have had enough education so they might go out and locate a job? But do you think anyone has a job for people like us? You see the prices yourself, you see the cost of living in a place as uncomfortable as this. How can they tell children that the country has jobs for them!

"Oh, I know what they want from us, I know it. I've been to the school meetings often enough to see what their officers are thinking about when they sit there looking at us. They are thinking, 'We never should have let you enter this country. We should have closed the doors when we first had a chance. We made the same mistake with the Indians and the Pakistanis. What were we thinking about when we let unskilled men arrive in this country?' But they took care of us, with our children. Mikko leave school and find a job? How could anyone take that as wise advice? A colored man in this country has his name on the bottom of every employment list, no matter what they say. Whites at the top, coloreds at the bottom. But it makes things better at the school for them. That is why they want it so. Too many children in a class, too much noise, no way to teach all the children in little rooms, no space, and the bigger ones make problems for them.

"Look at Mikko's friend, this Balassi. He's a criminal. I read about types like him. I do not associate with him. I lived my life to keep away from the Balassis. But school did it to him too. They spotted the boys who gave them trouble and told them to leave. Try, go on the train to London and look for jobs, they said. Girls too. Foolish, wasteful nonsense. And what chance did the parents of these children have with them hearing the advice of their *teachers* every day? It went through them, everything we tried to tell them. I had Mikko in here every night for three months. I told him on his fifteenth birthday that the most important act of his life was his education. But he had better ideas than his father. 'They don't do it like that here,' he told me, how many times! Where do you suppose he got these ideas, and his rudeness. From down there!" Frank Delano swung his arm around as if he wanted to punch a hole in the window. "And from that school of his. From that school. I know it.

"I'll tell you something, honest. Mikko is not smart enough to think up the idea of leaving school. He learned it from his teachers, he saw fate with his own eyes. He looked about that school, he looked about the schools where the rich send their children and he said to himself, 'What is my future if I stay here? What do I own at the end? I'll become like my father, wasting years, hunting for work where anyone with intelligence knows there cannot be work. And I don't want to end up like my father. I want it better.' And why shouldn't he have it better? Why should a son respect the steps of his father? Education is supposed to change that. My mother taught us that lesson forty-five years ago. No one falls upon money. A man works to find opportunities. But they sing differently now in these schools. They tell their children, go to work. That is how, don't you see, they control us, keep us in that part of the society and the part of the city where they like it best for us to be. It makes it nice for them. If Mikko finds his job, so much the better for him *and* the economy. But they know that Mikko will find nothing, I know. I know what there is for him to find. I have few skills, but I found something in my life. He has no skills, no skills. He has learned nothing in these schools. He learned as a child, in the beginning. We were excited. And he loved it. He was never late to his first school. But in the middle school we saw it changing.

"It has been this way with all the children. By the time they are nine or ten, the world closes down again, they have lost interest, the school has taught them how to lose interest, and it becomes very, very late for them. I have watched it happening with all my children. Bright babies, so much energy. And then in a few years they are changed people, as if we hadn't fed them properly, or let them have their exercise. It is the schools. They build their classes and that idea of leave-taking. Then the child fails on his own, you see what I mean, and the school can tell me, 'But it has nothing to do with us. Mikko chose to leave.' My son never chose such an action in his life. He follows orders. All the young follow orders; that is all they know. They follow orders of the television, their friends, their schools. Mainly the schools. They are being trained to see the uselessness of education. I call this a crime. It is disastrous. Eddie Balassi breaks into that store and walks right into the police. He has committed a crime and must be punished. Mikko is told to leave school, that they will find a place for him in the world, and anyway, they will take him back. All that is also a crime. But he does not walk into the police. It is worse for him, because he walks into nobody. No one is anywhere to help him or advise him. It would be better if a policeman found him and told him where he should be going. They stopped me and they will stop Mikko, then all his brothers and sisters.

"The test of the society is the schools, and our schools here are no better than what I knew. Maybe they are worse. This is a horrible admission, to myself, to realize that what I have tried to do in my life has brought me and seven other people just to this. There are times, you know, when I cannot bear the thought of it. I feel myself starting to cry. It goes nowhere, life, nowhere but where it started. The difference could be the schools, but, well, why talk about it. It must be boring to have to hear it. But who does one tell anymore? Who comes to us to listen? And they tell me on the telly that England might have a problem in the next few years. My God! What are the schools for? What's life for? What can I be certain about now? Anything at all?"

Thousands of London's young people now are officially considered 'school-leavers'. Not all of them, clearly, meet the same fate as Mikko Delano. But there are many presently caught between waves of inflation and unemployment who feel themselves going under. Their schools, they say, are not helping, but the schools have their own justification, their own sense of drowning in those infamous waves. Certainly it is in this context that the oppression of black people in England will continue to be seen. Maybe everybody knows about it, the world of Frank Delano and his family, the destiny of his children, the status of housing and medical care in Brixton, and of course the Brixton schools, no matter what the occasional utterances of certain politicians who prefer to look away, any way that keeps them from seeing the communities in Brixton. Maybe everyone knows. Mikko Delano does. He knows about the cricumstances of his life more and more, and as the days pass, his desire to speak about these circumstances increases.

It is almost one year that Mikko has not attended school. In all that time he has had jobs that total less than three weeks of work, and for some of those days he never received payment.

"What they did, see, was put me in one of their training programs. It was a job working for sheet goods. They have to train you, unless you know what they do, but how could anybody know. The man there, he was all right, he told me I start with a training program; then when I learn, they move me right into the job. I say to him, 'How long is the training program?' He doesn't know. 'Well, is it a week, a day, couple of years?' He doesn't know. 'How come you don't know?' I ask him. I'm not cross with the man. Maybe he doesn't know. Maybe he's new in his job like I'm new at my job, except I didn't really have a job yet. Finally, he says, 'Quite confusing, isn't it.' I say, 'Yeah, it's quite confusing.' I'm shaking my head too, because I have to know in my own mind, now what sort of a future do I have with a place like this that doesn't even know how long their own training program's going to be? Because I would have joined. I didn't care how long it would take. He didn't know I didn't have anything better. I would have taken it for sure. Why not?

"So he says finally, after all this time with the two of us just standing there looking at each other like a couple of dim animals, he says, 'I have to excuse myself about all this, but I don't know about the training program because we've never

had such a thing.' So I still don't care too much because I
didn't have any jobs when I went in to talk to the man, and I
sure didn't find any jobs while we were just standing there,
you know, looking at each other not sure what the other guy
was going to do. So I said, 'Take me. I'll learn.' So they did. I
went for the next four or five days. Got up early in the mornings like I was starting school all over again. My father felt
good seeing me do something. I felt pretty all right about myself. When you go to school, you really hate getting up every
morning. Especially me, because the whole last year or two I
kept asking myself, now what are you going to school for
when you know you aren't going to finish the place? I mean,
I knew I'd be one of the country's famous school-leavers, one
of the blokes you read about. School-leavers do this, school-
leavers do that. We always have the headlines, right? But then
when I got to be one of these famous school-leavers, I began
thinking, I sort of miss school. I mean, I wouldn't have missed
it if anybody gave me something productive to do. Anyway,
there I am, getting up early, smelling my father's aftershave,
you know, and it was kind of nice, 'specially the mornings
when we both went to work. I have to admit I liked that. He
went his way, I went my way, which was some way, I'll tell
you, 'cause it was almost fiftypence just to get there. I had to
go way to the other side of the city, but I didn't mind. I told
people I had a job. I didn't tell them I was just in a training
program. I mean, you don't like to leave school and tell people you're in a training program. 'Hey Delano, I understand
you're back in school. You should have finished.' That's what
they'd say, although most of my friends are doing the same
as me. They're all looking for work.

"I got one friend, Crater Bundle, honest to God that's his
name, Crater Bundle. This guy's been out of school eighteen
months and hasn't worked one day. And the guy has more
money than you could count. You want to know what he
does? He's a contact man for some international car stealing
ring. Honest to God. It's like he's in the movies, with his new
clothes, and he's always got some girl. He works for some
guy in, I don't know for sure, Kent, I think. They go around
switching license plates on cars and then ship them off, like
to the States or Australia; someone else works on forging papers. It's an enormous operation, and all this guy does is hunt
for makes of cars on the street and tells this other kid I know,
bloke named Fancy, that's what they call him since the birds

fancy him. Then Fancy steals the cars. It's fantastic. If I told those guys I'm working in sheet metal, in a training program, they'd laugh in my face. 'What's a matter, mate, you missing your little old school or something?' They'd say it, just like that too. 'What's a matter, Mikko?' So what am I supposed to do? Tell these characters with all their easy money that I'm in a stinker training program somewhere past Ealing? Hell no, man. I tell them I'm making all the money I need. Not that much, but all I need.

"My father always taught me you have to work and you have to be honest. You can have a job or be out of one, but you have to stay honest. There's never a reason to be dishonest. I mean, you have all these men out of work in the country, what are they doing? They're going into the street and in the pubs and they're talking. And what are they talking about? They're talking about ways they know or somebody somewhere else knows about making money. Men like that, you can be sure they hear all about different ways to make money, most of them pretty dishonest. So here you have my father telling me there's nothing wrong about being out of work. It's not what you want, but it's better than being in borstal. But I'm not so sure I agree with that. You take my situation. My school did nothing about my leaving, nothing in the world to stop me. They could have said something too, because I never went and said, I'm leaving and don't try to stop me. Then for four months I looked. July, August, September, and October. The sheet metal job came up on the last day of October. I started there in November. That's a lot of time to be doing nothing, man. A lot of time. I mean I'm not an old man with a few weeks to live. I was young. I still am.

"Okay, so I start and two weeks later, no, it's more like three weeks, this other man, not the one who talked to me the first time, comes to me and says, 'I just found out there is no training program.' 'What the hell you talking about, man?' I wanted to belt him. 'There's no training program.' 'So where's the job?' 'No job.' 'You telling me I been working here three weeks, ain't got a shilling from you and there's no job? No program?' 'That's it.' I'll tell you something. We were talking, this man and me, Mr. Mackenzie was his name, and next to him on this table where I was working, there was this big sheet-metal shears. Most of the time you have to use both hands to cut with them, and they keep those blades razor sharp. I saw these shears lying there, couldn't be two feet from where I was. I said to myself, 'Take that shears, you sod, and wrap them around that man's neck. Then tell him, he wants his head where it is, he gets you the job.' I saw myself stabbing the poor guy with it. I was mad, man, like I never knew I could be.

"There was this other man there, nice man named Kingman. We never said much to each other. First time I saw him I said to myself, this person can't stand West Indians, Pakistanis, Indians, nobody colored. But I don't know. I think maybe he was just a quiet guy. But he taught me a lot, everything I learned there. Like he would have been a real good teacher. But he saw me looking at the shears, and real quietly he stepped in there, you know, and took them away like he was going to use them himself. You could see he didn't want the other man there to know what I was thinking about. I might have done it. I might have gotten off on that Mackenzie man long enough to shove those shears right through his heart, even though it wasn't his fault. Kingman knew.

"I didn't do anything but tell them to send my money to my home. No, first I asked for it there but they said it took time and they'd send it. They never did. I worked three weeks and never got anything. You think that's fair? Maybe they did and maybe they didn't have a training program. I'll never know. But they screwed me out of what I had coming. That night I told my parents. You should have seen my father, and heard him. 'Yeah, and what'd you do?' he said exactly ten million times. 'I didn't do nothing. Honest to God,' I told him. 'Nobody gets promised like that and doesn't get payed.' 'Call them yourself,' I said. 'I will. Don't you worry, I will. So big school-leaver, what do you plan to do about all this now? What do you have next on the list?' 'I ain't got anything,' I told him. 'I'll look again.' 'You stay away from Balassi and those criminals.' That's the last thing he said. After saying ten million times, 'What did *you* do, what did *you* do,' he ends up telling me to stay away from Eddie Balassi, which I was going to do anyway because if I was thinking about doing something in the rackets, you can be damn sure I'm not doing anything with a common thief. Balassi is a nobody, man. He was never anything. So when I told my father I'd stay away from guys like that, I was telling the truth. *That* time I was telling the truth. I told myself that night, I was walking around by myself, you know, near Battersea Park somewhere, I said to myself, I'm going to look for jobs exactly three more months. The first of February, I quit looking if nothing comes up. And no second-rate job; nobody's going to give me a little present; it's a real job or no job at all. They got gifts for all us famous school-leavers, you know. Running errands for people, or shining cars. I said no to all that. It's got to be real.

"What men like my father don't want to understand is that moving into this country isn't any game. I mean, you can't hassle me about being here, you know what I mean. That's my father's game. That's the battle he fought. I'm English. I'm entitled to all this, the best school, a job, the whole thing, just like everybody else. But they don't see it that way, I guess. They got this idea that the coloreds, that's us, we're just used to being second class. But I can be just as angry with my father about this as anybody else. The way I see it, it's too late in the game for him to be telling me how the most important thing is to be honest. I told myself at Battersea that night, I got three more months of being honest and that is the end, the limit. I got no job, no prospects, nothing lined up. My school hasn't taught me anything I can use. So where am I in the world? And where am I supposed to go? You know what a friend of mine told me once, and she was dead right? I told her she was crazy, but she was right. She said school should have taught us how to speak French and Italian and some of these other languages so we could go to those countries and look for work. Makes sense if you think of it. But the only thing my father had to tell me was stay out of trouble, be honest, come home early every night, and tell me everything you're doing. Tell him everything I'm doing? That ain't the way to stay close to your son. 'I'm stealing cars, dad. Now aren't you glad I told you?' 'Yeah, son, just as long as I know.' I ain't going to tell him what I'm doing when I know just as well as he does what I'm doing is about the worst thing I could be doing. What am I going to tell him for? Hell, if I told him what I found, he'd have called the police in on me faster than they would have found me without his help. Crazy, the way it turns out for some people, isn't it? Crazy's the only word they got for it too."

Mikko Delano did count the months as he said he would. He pursued whatever employment leads arose, although there were few, almost hoping that nothing would come of them. The pursuit of work, once a sort of game with him, now had become an intense personal battle. He had grown convinced that the system of education, the country, the world had let

him down. The proof of this contention was the absence of
jobs. If something arose, a real job, one that showed promise for him, his entire perspective of the country his father had chosen for him, would have been changed. As it was, he detested the circumstances in which he had grown up, and with each rebuke claimed to hate his father that much more.

"No job, no chances, no future," he said with bitterness one afternoon, after he had waited four hours to see a prospective employer who never turned up. "Standing around in an office waiting for someone who isn't even there. Has his secretary tell people he's coming in any minute, any minute. What an incredible lie. They put adverts in for jobs but the jobs don't exist anywhere. They aren't anywhere. My father says it's because we're colored. Maybe so. I used to think it. I still think it. I don't know what to think about it. There were ten white blokes in there today, sitting there just like me. They never saw the man either, so it looks on that one we're all getting it.

"I'll tell you who the fool is. The fool is my father. He never did anything good in his life. First mistake was to leave the islands. All right, he did it and he found work in the States, so why didn't he stay? He had it made there, so why'd he move? Then he moves again and comes here. Then he sees he can't get work here, why'd he stay? Why'd he stay? So his children have to have it as bad as he did? So is he happy? Now he hates all of us for leaving school, as if that would have made a difference in this whole thing. I don't understand the guy. I really don't. But I'll tell you for sure, I sat in that man's office this morning waiting for a job interview—that's even becoming a great thing these days, just to talk to the guy that says 'Go 'way, kid' —and I don't hate that man. I should, but I don't. I don't hate him 'cause *he* didn't put me in that room with all those other characters like me. My *father* put me in that room, just as sure as if he dragged me in there with me kicking and screaming. *He's* the one this country should have talked to, a long time ago.

"My father always tells this story, you know, he'll tell it to anybody. All about how he came to England and how people here looked at him like he really had no business coming here, you know. How he should have stayed where he was, which people around here always think has to be Africa. People here, you know, they want to keep their little empire just like it's always been, nice and pure and white and all that. Coloreds come in, they get so confused most of the time they think we're all from Africa. Anyway, my father tells his little story about how even though no one wanted him, he stayed, and worked, and took everything people threw at him, like he was some brave soldier. That's the way he wants people to see him, like some big general who beat the enemy with only ten of his men and ten thousand of the enemy. My father didn't get *anywhere* in this country. He didn't get anywhere in this little bit of a community and we aren't even living in the main part of London either. So what has he done that he walks around with so much pride? I say he's done nothing but make a couple of bad mistakes, like where he lives and where he sent us to school, and a million other things I could name if I wanted to. He's put me in this position; no one else. I could blame the country and all their stupid policies, but I'm holding back. I'll give myself a few more months. A few more months, then we'll see."

The winter and spring brought no jobs. Mikko Delano's relationship with his father had grown worse, to the point where they rarely talked. But Frank Delano could understand his son's frustration. He kept by his word that it was not his son who chose to leave school, but that the boy had been encouraged by his teachers. He lectured Mikko during the few minutes the boy would sit still, about running around with criminal types like Eddie Balassi, but Mikko would only shake his head as if to say, I'm tired of that speech, can't you come up with a better one. "You got a thing about Eddie Balassi," he told his father one night. "I don't see Eddie Balassi, I don't want to see him, I don't care whether he dies. You ask anyone you like whether Mikko Delano runs around with Eddie Balassi. Go ahead. You afraid to find out?"

"Don't tell me what to do," Frank roared at his son. "If I want to check up on you, I will feel perfectly free to do that too."

"Hey, that's great," Mikko muttered, looking at his mother who remained silent in the corner of the room. "I get to have police watching out for me on the outside and my father checking out on all the things the police might miss. That the idea of freedom you love so much?"

"You should be whipped," Frank said sternly. "You should be cracked across the mouth. You're going to end up rotten if you keep going like this. You're going to end up so rotten it will make you sick and there'll be nothing I'll do. Nothing I will even want to do. No, you aren't running around with

Eddie Balassi. You're running around with a hundred Eddie Balassis. A million for all I know. And what they're doing to your mind makes me sick!"

"What about not being able to work? What does that do for me?"

"I lived with it," Frank answered his son smartly. "I had to put up with it, and have all my responsibilities. What responsibilities do you have? Suppose you tell me. You look for work. All right. That's hard. Very hard. But you eat, don't you? You have a place to sleep. So what is your problem that you've grown to be so *tough*, like a little gangster, so tough, tough?"

"Man, if you don't know by now, I pity you." Mikko Delano was spitting out the words. That his mother was crying and his father seething didn't stop him in the slightest. "If you don't even read the newspapers to find out what kids like me are going through now, I pity you. What the hell you think this is all about, man? You think this is a game I'm playing, running all over this city begging people to make up work for me to do? Deliver little parcels for them or wipe up floors? You think it's going to get better, suddenly the government's going to hand down a million new jobs for people? You know what they got planned? They got this thing so worked out it makes me sick. They got a plan that all the little colored kids, we're told to leave school and think about jobs and making money. Then you know what happens? A few of us get our little rotten work so we're helping them, right? But most of us, we don't get anything. You don't have a million Eddie Balassis running around down there, you got ten million Mikko Delanos! They know they got us and the only thing we're going to do for them is get thrown in jail or get on a ship and get the hell out of this country, out of their sight, and that's exactly what they want us to do. If you think all that is nothing more than a game, then that's fine with me, but *you* don't have to play it."

Frank Delano looked at his wife who was crying but nodding her head in agreement with her son. "You believe that nonsense?" he shouted at her. "You believe him?"

"You're damn right she does," Mikko impetuously answered for his mother.

"I wasn't talking to you," his father reprimanded him.

"Sorry boss," Mikko muttered under his breath.

"I don't know what to believe," Miriam said softly, as if she were about to give up living. "He sounds like he knows what he's talking about. Not working, not going to school, it's hard on him. It's hard on all of us, but it's hardest on him. It's *his* life." Her strength was coming back and she wanted her son to know he had her support. But if Mikko Delano appreciated her concern, he did not acknowledge it. He never bothered to look at her, but waited, head bowed, for his father's stern reprimand. His mother waited for it too.

Frank Delano looked back and forth between his wife and his son. Several times he drew in his breath as if he were about to speak, but each time he changed his mind and remained silent. After several minutes he walked out of the room. Mikko looked up, surprised, then left the house.

Wherever he went, Mikko Delano's activities were known to no one in his family, not even Charlie who normally knew everything his brother did. They all assumed the young man remained on his course of hunting for jobs. But Mikko had given up any hope of finding work. Instead, he had become friendly with Crater Bundle, a twenty year old with big hands and the most convincing way of speaking Mikko had ever heard. Everybody said the same thing about Crater Bundle. He had a funny name, strong hands that broke your own when he shook hands, and a way of talking that could charm anyone. He also had what he called the sweetest game in town. With boys like Mikko out of work, he had no trouble finding new recruits. The car theft ring to which Crater belonged seemed to be the perfect business. While Mikko never understood the details, and particularly the way money was kept in special accounts, Crater made Mikko believe that nothing could go wrong. The amount of work might come to three or four hours a week, and for that he could earn up to one hundred quid a week. At first Mikko didn't like the idea, but as there was nothing else, he joined up with Crater Bundle and six other youths, none of whom ever met the men who ran the organization. Crater claimed no one knew them, but he would speak to people on the telephone now and again who presumably gave him orders. Mikko Delano learned quickly to ask no questions of anyone.

His job for the organization was simple. He was to prowl streets looking for any car that had been left with the keys in it. He was not to break into any car. Other boys did this. If he went weeks without finding cars with keys, he received no money. He was paid only for delivering the cars to certain garages. The job was so easy he laughed when he thought about it. Then one night he drove away in a new Jaguar with his friend Billy Sansolo, the two of them screaming with delight and excitement at the thrill of sitting in the front seat of one of the finest cars on the road. The motor purred like a cat, and the boys ran their hands over the leather upholstery. With Mikko driving, it was Billy's task to hunt through the car to see if he could find the owner's name. The search ended immediately when in the glove compartment he found a wallet belonging to a judge. Whereas many people who discovered their car stolen soon gave up their hunt for it and settled instead for the insurance money, a judge, the boys reasoned, would not do the same. He would have the police involved as soon as possible.

Mikko Delano felt frightened for the first time since he began stealing cars. Billy Sansolo couldn't have cared less. "Who's to know?" he said to his friend. "One job's just like all the others. What the hell, we don't know whose car we've stolen each time. We might have half the MP's cars in our stables for all we know."

Mikko was not satisfied, but the handsome gray Jaguar was delivered to the garage, and the young mechanics, all of them hired and screened by Crater Bundle, broke out into applause and shouts when they saw it. In twenty-four hours everything about the car was to be changed, all identifying parts altered. It was a dark brown Jaguar that was being prepared for shipment to the United States. Forged owner's papers would accompany it. In New York a man posing as the owner would run an advertisement. Good as new Jaguar for sale, the advert would read. Owner suddenly leaving the country, willing to strike bargain. Crater Bundle's boys loved the line about the owner suddenly leaving the country. As for the bargain, it was perfectly true. The new owner benefitted greatly. Crater's mechanics left their cars in magnificent shape. And all the money was profit. The plan and the execution were superb, except this one time.

Mikko Delano had been right to worry about a distinguished judge's reaction to his car being stolen. The police were called in, squads of them. Then someone in Mikko's neighborhood was arrested for breaking into a hardware store, and he talked about every criminal activity he had ever heard of. Mikko's name wasn't mentioned but another of Crater's boys was. Teddy "the Pub" Petrone was fingered, and to save his own skin, Teddy gave the police the addresses of some of the garages. Crater Bundle knew of Teddy talking and cleared every-thing out of the garage except the judge's Jaguar. The police found it, half grey, half brown, with only one of its original tires. They also found Billy Sansolo's fingerprints all over the car, for the boy had forgotten to wear his gloves until he be-gan fishing for the identity of the car's owner. Billy Sansolo was in police custody less than three hours after Teddy Petrone had told his story. Then Billy talked too. He described the operation of the gang, but said he knew only two people; one of them was Mikko Delano. He said later that he gave the po-lice Mikko's name to help his friend, who he thought would be straightened out by a time in borstal. Mikko, he said, was thinking too much about crime.

In the end, Teddy Petrone, Billy Sansolo, and Mikko De-lano were sentenced to serve time in borstal. For the first sev-eral months, Mikko was so upset by what had happened, he refused to talk to anyone. He was a model prisoner, obeying to the letter every law of the borstal, but the boys learned early that he was not one to talk. In time his anger receded and he began looking forward to visits with friends and mem-bers of his family, and especially with his father.

Frank Delano was disturbed by his son being sent to bor-stal, but he was neither surprised nor vindictive. He knew his son's chances as well as Mikko did; he knew there would be no jobs and that Mikko's falling in with boys already in the rackets was an inevitability. The magnitude of the crime, its international scope, was somewhat of a shock to Frank De-lano, but even this, he told himself, should have been expect-ed. The times change, Mikko, he said. It was not an immigrant from the Islands going out begging for work.

His son had used the same words. Sitting at a long table on which the boys ate their meals, in a huge room now empty except for a small booth that served as a custodian's office, Mikko Delano spoke of his life. His manner was one of a per-son in a hurry. He had nothing to do for more than an hour, but he was eager to be finished with this conversation, and with many other things as well.

"I don't go begging for work. I didn't when I started, and I won't when I get out. I'll pinch cars again if I have to. I'll look for the same guys, the same way of life if I have to. How's all this going to change me? Two years in here? What's it go-ing to do for me? Is it going to get me a job? You think that's what's going to happen? So I know some carpentry now that

I didn't know before. Big deal! I can push two by tens through
a table saw eight hours a day and end up every night with ten
fingers. Who's going to hire me when I get out? A school-leaver with a record? Jesus, if I was ending up with nothing before, I'll get double nothing now. At least I remember *that*
from school: two times naught is naught! Pretty great, ain't
it? I'm doing just what my father had in mind, ain't I. Man,
have I let him down. He comes here to see me but doesn't say
anything to me. No more lectures like he always did. We just
kill a few minutes together. I damn near cry every time he
leaves. It's so pitiful. His life was bad enough without him
having to worry about me. My mother too, I've given her a
lot of grief. I wish they knew how sorry I am about that. I
think about them all the time. I think about school too, and
all the great things they never got around to doing for me
there. But I can't sit here, in this hole of a place, as bad as it
is—and this place is really the worst—and say I'll get out of
here and never come back. I don't know where Sansolo is, if
he's in borstal or out. But he'll be out when I get out, that's
for sure, and I'm going after him. I'll tell you that too. Most
guys, they'll talk, like in the shop, how when they get out
for a weekend or a day pass, how they're going to see their
mother and get a big dinner. Not me. I'm going after Sansolo.
When that's done, then I'll see my parents and have a big dinner.

"You know, that's a funny thing, I just thought. Most everybody here, they either got one parent or they live with just
one. Almost nobody here I talked about it with has both parents. Most of these guys, they don't even know where their
father is, if they ever knew their father. 'Course lots of them
know their fathers, only they don't like talking about them
so they say they're dead or run off somewhere. That guy who
just walked through here before, tall thin guy with the long
nose, he told me once how he never even knew his father. Man
walked out on his family, six kids, when he was like a year old.
Can't even remember his father. Doesn't even know if he *ever*
saw him, for that matter. Sad story, right? You know what I
heard from the doctor? Doctor told me the guy was working
in the rackets from the time he was nine years old. Nine years
old! And you know who he's working for all that time, like
more than ten years? His old man! His *father*! And that guy's
going around telling everybody how they should feel sorry for
him 'cause he doesn't have parents. He sees his father every

day. His father visits him here and they do business and he still doesn't tell anybody it's his father.

"Most guys, though, they got broken families. Not many like me, bad eggs coming from a good family. I'm not proud of that. Neither is my father, I suppose. I guess nobody could be. I ruined things for my father, or made a bad thing really bad. I can't say I'm done and mean it. I don't know how I'm going to feel when I get out of here, but if Sansolo is around, I'll have to do something. I can't swallow that. My father knows that too. I've swallowed too much already; there's no more room in my mouth. Maybe I'll change. I doubt it though. Two, three years in here is one helluva long time, but I don't know if it's enough to make me change, about Sansolo and the rackets I mean. I suppose if I came out of here and a man met me up there on Felton Road, you know, with a job, a good job that made me feel they weren't just making up something out of the air, I suppose maybe I'd think about Sansolo all over again. Maybe I wouldn't either. I'd like my father to see me doing something worthwhile once in my life. But if there was a job, that'd have to change my head a little.

"What I think about all the time is that none of this is my fault. I didn't choose to live where we live, or have my father out of work as much as he's been, or the school I went to. I didn't choose any of those things; anybody can see how much they made me what I am. I guess I did choose to leave school; that has to be the number one bad decision maybe, but everybody else was doing it. Nobody said not to do it. Now they got thousands like me doing it. Nobody knows what's going to happen to them. If they aren't careful in this country, they'll have to turn all the space into borstals. Anyway, that's what I think, that it isn't my fault. But then I think, maybe it is. Maybe when the crunch came I could have made up my mind the other way. Like, if I don't find a job after ten years, I'll kill myself, or drink myself to death, but I won't go into the rackets. Do it that way you don't make no trouble for the government. They just throw your body out. Probably don't even bother to identify you. Or if they do, they probably don't tell your parents, and that takes care of that, nice and simple. Lovely way to go out. This way, I soak up the money doing time in here. One way or another, I got the government spending some money on me. That's right too. I cost them sitting in here. Right this minute, sitting at this table doing nothing is costing one of those offices a few quid.

I'll bet it comes down to a couple quid an hour too, just to keep me healthy and pretty to look at while I'm sitting here. You'd think they'd be better off giving me a job for all that money. Or better yet, making the schools better. I never thought of it until just now, but at my age I'm supposed to still be in school. Right this minute, that's where I'm supposed to be, not here. God only knows, my father only knows. I only know. Not here!"

Part Three

**Observations
of Adults**

To listen to the media and to certain scholars' interpretations of their research, one might get the impression that from every standpoint, the American family is disintegrating. What seems to make news and arouse the fascination of so many people are stories of divorce, family feuds, child abuse, abandonment, generational tensions, and even the separation of people from relatives outside the nuclear family. The statistics of demise are omnipresent. The stories of loving, caring family involvements are rarely told; when they are, people are victimized by romanticization and exaggeration, and decent hard-working, caring human beings are portrayed as two-dimensional, uninteresting, flat.

During the last ten years of research, I have befriended several hundred poor families, some of them with as many as fourteen and fifteen children. Those who understand the patterns of family life in these communities—if indeed one can accurately speak of patterns—know that divorce and child abuse and tensions of all sorts exist under these circumstances. They know too, that family members on occasion kill each other. Indeed, this fact seems to be known by everybody, although the conditions under which these families survive are not known by everybody. In these communities there are a great many human beings working extraordinarily hard to preserve the integrity and dignity of their families. They know that three or four generations of people, people whose backgrounds are so varied it is difficult to believe they could be parents and children to one another, are living together and watching out for one another in the most noble expression of kinship. And they know that this effort to reaffirm family ties is no small matter when families are limited in the amount of visiting they can do.

Some observers claim that poor families disintegrate at an especially high rate. My own impression is that the rate of disintegration and lack of involvement simply is not to be found in the way in which some observers construe it. What is true is that the everyday, unending reality of poverty, and such programs as aid to dependent children and the welfare system, make it almost impossible for individuals, let alone family units, to survive. Yet some families do more than survive. They conduct their lives in a fashion that pleases society, and along the way, not only watch out for their relatives, some of whom they have surpassed in terms of social standing and economic success, but also keep in touch with family members everywhere. They keep in touch with the old ones, the young ones, the newest ones. They even keep in touch with the dead ones, for they have learned that maintaining family ties requires that one rely on memory as well as letter writing; one pays respect to deceased parents and grandparents in the ways life is led each day.

What follows is a conversation with a woman I have known for four years. We met when a cousin of hers introduced us and since that time I have visited with her quite regularly in her home, although on many occasions I have accompanied her and her children on shopping trips and excursions. I cannot say that this woman is typical, because I am often troubled by that word, typical. I suspect that it is partly a desire to generalize from the words of one person that makes us regard that person as typical. So I can't proclaim that this one woman is typical, even knowing that other people look out for their families as she does, and make certain that their particular kinship stays intact. I know, too, that there are more people than we can imagine, more people than we think about or hear about, who conduct their lives like this one woman.

I must confess, however, that in the beginning I found it hard to believe that well over a hundred people in the Jenkins family keep in contact. In parts of the family, four generations survive, and for a household of Jenkins or Purchases, Rowes, Gables, Silbeys—or whatever their names are now after all those marriages—to have three surviving generations is nothing at all. Jenkins people have been saying for years that it would take a whole university of historians to trace their family back in time, and the whole FBI to locate every Jenkins alive now in the United States. "If anybody ever did the proper study," Pearl Jenkins once said, "they'd probably discover five hundred cousins and aunts and uncles living maybe in every state there is."

Pearl Jenkins would know too, for she has kept in contact with a great number of her relatives. "Probably keep a bunch of the families together," is the way she has described her interest in these people. She receives four or five letters a week from persons wanting to know the whereabouts of a relative, or someone announcing the birth of a baby or the graduation of a young man or woman. It is an exceptional role that this thirty-eight-year-old woman maintains. Every other day she threatens to abandon the whole idea and forget everyone in the world named Jenkins, but then a note will come in the

mail and reawaken her involvement in the family. Several
times she has promised to publish the material she has collected but then she modestly backs down. "Well, we're really only important to each other. Just 'cause a family wants to know
about relatives scattered around here and there don't mean
that other folks care too much. Fact is, I bet if you ask folks,
they wouldn't want to know anything about us."

Perhaps Pearl Jenkin's most interesting observations of her
family involve the changes from generation to generation and
the transformations within individual families, especially her
own.

"Start with my father. 'Course, I could go back farther,
probably find you all the slave laborers you'd ever want to
know about. Had a great uncle once who belonged to what
they claimed was the largest plantation in Georgia. He was
supposed to be a very fine man. I'd loved to have known him.
Almost could have too, 'cause I think he lived past a hundred.
But look here at my father." She removed a photograph that
had been pasted inside a book, and held it up. "That was a
proud, hard-working man. Long as anyone knew him he believed in working ten hours a day, six days a week. Would have
worked on Sundays too, except the neighbors probably would
have boxed his ears back. He and my mother worked this little postage stamp farm in Arkansas. Beautiful brown earth. I
remember his clothes always smelled of it.

"Funny thing about my father. No matter how hard he
worked, and no matter how much his back or legs might have
ached him— at the end of his life he was carrying on in lots of
pain—he never complained. Just kept on working. Almost
thought I saw a little smile on his face when he worked those
few acres they had. Never complained about the weather. If
it rained, he just waited for it to stop. If it got cold, he just
started his planting all over again. It was like the land was his
real family, and all those plants he cared for, his real children.
Fact is, if you step back to look at it, he might have been a
whole lot kinder to that land than he was to his children. He
could be tough with the eight of us. Each one got it if he went
out of line. I'll give him that. He was fair. No one got a special
favor, but whoa, could he lay the law on us. That was it too,
you know. My daddy's law. Country might have had *its* laws,
but in our house you obeyed my daddy's law or you paid the
price. Treated my mother the same way. When things were going good, he treated us fine, but when something went wrong,

like the time he once blamed my mother 'cause he thought she was responsible for breaking the plumbing, then he'd be the toughest one. You didn't argue back when I was a child. You just stood there, heard him out, and either walked away with your chin up or your chin down, crying tears. Lots of children, you know, they'll laugh when they see their brother or sister getting it from their daddy. They're just scared, probably a little happy too that nothing happened to them. But in my family, there wasn't no one who laughed at a punished child. When someone was the victim of my father's law, everyone got to know just how that felt, so no one laughed.

"Now my mother, she couldn't have been more unlike my father. First off, she was a whole lot smaller than he was, but she was strong. Lots of times I felt her arms and they were hard, like iron rods. She worked all her life too, field work, same as he did. Put in the same ten hours like him, only she didn't have no rest on Sundays. I can close my eyes and see my mother doing everything around that farm, milking, hauling, turning over the dirt with this red pitchfork my daddy painted special for her. He gave it to her, I remember. Told her there wasn't any sense him getting her ladies things 'cause they'd never see the day when she'd get to wearing them. But I saw her in all those poses, and never once do I remember that woman sitting down to rest. She was out of her bed, washed and dressed before any of the children got up and never went to bed before us, even when we were grown up. Never even saw her lie down for a minute to take a break. I'll bet the first time she ever lay down to rest when the sun was shining was the last days in the hospital, right before she died. I remember my daddy saying to her how she looked funny lying down in the middle of the day. It was true, too. His day started at 4 A.M. Her's did too. Stayed that way for both of them up until the time they died. Everybody said she'd way outlive him the way he worked, but she didn't. It wasn't no surprise that he followed her three years later.

"They were good people. He was tough, putting down the law, like I said, and she was soft. When you wanted soft you went to her. When you needed something, like money or to get something material, you went to him. Made it easy for us. When one of the children would have some kind of problem, it was pretty easy to know who to talk to. You better know, too, that we behaved. Maybe once we'd get out of hearing distance out beyond the road, we'd scream to wake up the devil. But when mother and daddy could hear, or when they'd be walking with us, like to church on Sundays, then you saw the best behaved children in all of Arkansas. It even surprised me to see my brothers, who the teachers couldn't turn off no matter what they tried, walking so nicely, not too fast and not too slow neither, and talking so quietly. My daddy just didn't see that there was any reason for anybody to be misbehaving. 'Ain't no wordly reason for it,' was his favorite expression. Old Ronnie would be walking a bit too fast and my father would jump ahead and pull him back and say 'There ain't no wordly reason for that!' Ronnie didn't argue. No one dared argue with him.

"What's more, we were clean. Something else my daddy used to say was that folks who work in the field had no good reason to be running around dirty. 'No sense bragging about your working on the land,' he'd say. 'When you're done, you get clean. Anyone who shows his dirt probably isn't working that hard.' My mother agreed with him. If a man came to the door all filthy from working in the field, the first question you'd want to ask him is, how come he's standing at your door instead of working where he's supposed to? My daddy made us wash before every meal. When he didn't say nothing, my mamma did. I did the same thing with my children. 'You can't make 'em look rich,' my mother always said, 'but when you take 'em out with you, you sure can make 'em look clean.'

"Looking back at it, my mother could be a little tough, I suppose, in her way, but I think if you asked my brothers and sisters they'd say they obeyed my father out of fear and my mother 'cause she treated us nice. I don't mean he wasn't nice, but when he'd come into the house you sure could tell it got a whole lot quieter."

When Pearl Jenkins was twenty, she married William Tanker, an employee of the telephone company. A lot had happened since the days on the farm in Arkansas. Her father, Charles Jenkins, had died, and three of the children (Pearl and two brothers) had come north after spending several months in Memphis. Pearl's brother Ossie got married soon after leaving Tennessee; her other brother Clifford stayed in Boston a few years, then returned to the South and settled in Greensboro. It was his move that got Pearl interested in tracking down her relatives.

After a few years, William Tanker and his wife were living in a small house in a Boston suburb. By the time Pearl was thirty, she had three sons and a daughter, children, she claims, who couldn't care less about the way she and her own brothers and sisters had been raised.

"I keep telling them they'll want to know someday. 'You don't have to know nothing about history now, but you'll be begging me one of these days.' They say they don't have much interest in Arkansas farms. I don't much blame them, although it's always seemed to me that a person ought to know something about his roots. There's a connection, I tell them, between my daddy working a field near Helena and your daddy working for the phone company here, but they don't see it. So damn much has changed it's hard to believe all of it's happened in just one lifetime. I can't believe that my life could be so different from my mother's. It's not that many years, and here I am with a dishwasher and TV. Hell, we got a two-car garage. Only got but one car, but we're all ready if we could ever afford another one. My father didn't even have a shed for his machinery and tools. Used to lean 'em up against the side of the house and cover 'em with a big hunk of canvas. And here we are sitting with a two-car garage. If you're looking down at us, Daddy, be sure you know we got room for you.

"'Course lots of things are a whole lot better now. You take a man's working hours. William's never home past 6:30. Sometimes he comes home in the afternoon too. He spends more time with the children in one weekend than my father could spend with us in a month. And we get vacations, when he's with the children all the time. I ain't worked outside this house in almost five years. I don't put no time in for Ma Bell or sweep up no lady's house. I mean I've worked. Isn't any family of our status where the woman gets to sit home all the time. But work like my mother? Not a chance. I'm a princess next to the way that woman was meant to live.

"Strange, but I can see a big difference between my mother and me. She worked all the time, never thought to sit down. You don't have to do what she did to know how tired a person gets working every hour except the hours when she was in church, not that I ever caught that woman in church with her eyes closed. My daddy slept there, but my mother's eyes were wide open, looking back and forth between her children and the minister. Still, as tired as she was, she never really got mad at her children, the type of mad I mean, when you think you're about to go beyond the bend. He could scare the liv-

ing and dying hell out of us, but she had a way of keeping herself together even when she was her most tired and beaten
self. But me, I ain't got no work outside this house. I got a
husband who'd bring Colonel Sanders in with *all* his chickens
if I asked him to. All I say is, I ain't up to cooking tonight,
bring me the Colonel. So I ain't got a real complaint. I never
even take out the garbage, and *I* get mad at my children. I
mean I steam at 'em, spit fire, scare the hell out of 'em same
as my daddy did.

"It's hard to understand. I guess one generation makes all
that difference. Take another thing. I do school committee
work. I do neighborhood welcoming work when new folks
move in. I even get involved with some of the political campaigns. Now here I am working to make sure folks are all reg-
istered, and in all their days my mother and father never voted
once. I remember hearing the elections on the radio when I
was small, or sitting around watching them on TV. But when
I'd ask my father what he was going to do, he'd just walk
away. He talked about politics. Wouldn't take anything for
him to start arguing about conditions. But voting? Not if
they promised him a new car. Never thought it would do any
good. I'd love to know what he'd think if he saw me working
at the registration office. I just wonder what he'd say.

"We had more than twenty folks here the other night talking about getting the town to go back to two garbage collections a week. You hear that? They used to have two collections
before we came out here and now they want it again. With
the taxes we pay, why should all that stuff just sit there smelling up the yard and collecting flies? Let 'em come out here a
second time and pick it up again. We'll drag the barrels out
there for them if that's what they want. The deal all those
unions got. What they really should be doing is coming into
all these backyards and taking those barrels out there for us
in the first place.

"You see what's burdening me? I had a mother and father
had their lives cut short by working from early in the morning to late at night just to eat. Still have a brother and sister
living in the poorest conditions you'd ever want to see, and
here I'm serving on a committee to get the garbage folks to
come out here Mondays and Thursdays instead of just Mondays. I'll bet my father would pull out his belt if he saw what
kinds of things I was doing with my time. I don't remember
garbagemen coming at any time in my life. I don't think I

saw garbage collected 'til we moved to Memphis. Now I'm on the garbage committee. Everybody's waiting to hear me speak. Sound just like all the rest of 'em too. 'Bring 'em out here two days a week and let 'em do all the carrying. If they're big enough to lift the stuff and dump it in the truck, they're big enough to carry the cans out from the yard.' I don't believe the kind of stuff I hear myself talking about half the time. My father heard me talking like this, he'd beat me. I know he would.

"But see, even though only a few years have gone by, changes are happening all the time. It doesn't go slow anymore like it used to. Ten years now is like a lifetime when my grandparents were alive, half a lifetime when my parents were alive. Nobody can afford to wait no more. You wait and you miss out on too much. Like education. There was no one when we were children who made us believe education counted for anything. It was like my father and his attitudes about voting. No one cared. A person could tell you every day of your life you had to study, do well in school, but no one would have believed him. Problem was, we didn't see no one ever benefiting from school. All our education was at home. My mother made us work at our books after school, but there wasn't any reason to do it. We all knew no one would finish. Hell, the high school was nine miles away and the bus took over an hour with all the stops it made. Even if you got it you were late to school by an hour and they punished you. When the weather was bad you couldn't walk and my daddy liked to keep the boys home anyway to help him. So we quit. I went up to eighth grade which wasn't so bad compared to most of the other children who lived near us. You'd think they might have cared a little bit in those schools whether we went or not, but they didn't. You stopped going and that was it. No one called up your mother to ask whether you were sick or dead or gone away. They were just as glad we weren't going anymore.

"Maybe that attitude has changed. William and me picked this place mostly because we knew we could find good schools here. It's like I say, things change. My kids won't stop going. College, too, if they want. Times change, and places change. Another thing that's different is the way we plan for our children, teach them to think about their futures. Where I came from, it was enough just to hope your children wouldn't have to live the way you did the rest of their lives. No one was going anywhere in the society, but some folks could arrange to have their children get out. See what I'm saying? But that's not true anymore. Least for folks like us. We're making our children think about careers. When I grew up there was only the day you were living to be thinking about. There was no use wondering about tomorrow. It'd be the same or you'd be gone or dead. Your job was to get through the days, one at a time. My husband and me, we get ourselves and our children through the days, the weeks, the months, the years too. And the reason we're doing it this way's so that *our* children can spend all their time getting ready for the future. We'll carry 'em as long as we can, don't you see. As long as they need us. When I was a child, nobody carried nothing for nobody. You barely had time to carry the babies. More likely you'd be setting them down somewhere and moving on with your chores. Lots of time now. Years go by quick, but everyday I know I can make just a little bit of time for myself. So like I say, we're moving out and up a little, and my children are going to be moving up even higher.

"I don't suppose anyone knows for sure where their children are going to end up. Most important thing is that they're good children, that they treat other folks good. My mother and daddy would have said the same for us. Not everything has changed that much. Everybody wants their children to be good, but when you start moving up a little in this country and you begin tasting those sweet tastes of making it, you need more, for yourself and your children too. You want them still to be good, but you want more for them too. Good marriages, good houses, making good money, a position in the society. They ought to be somebody beyond what they are by nature of just being alive. I like to dream of my children even being celebrities. Kind of when you mention their names people would know who you were talking about. My father always said every person on the earth was a special person. I know he meant it. But I used to hear him talking, when he didn't think the rest of us were listening, that rich folks were special and that farm folks weren't. He knew that no one in our family was really special, no matter how much he tried to preach to us about it. Nobody's special when they're poor. But I see my children growing up to be special. Lots of things standing in their way, but they got the right sort of chances. You won't find them worrying where tomorrow's supper's coming from like my father did, or how to play the ADC organization. They're going to move higher up. I'd like to see it too.

"Every time I talk this way though, I get a funny idea coming into my head. Here we are, living so far beyond our parents' means, breaking our necks in old America so that we might live a little easier and make it all right for our children. But every once in a while I get this idea that my children are going to come to me some day with their bags all packed, dressed up real nice, you know, and say that they've decided what they're going to do in the future. 'What's that?' I'll ask, thinking they're about to let me in on some beautiful surprise. 'Well,' they'll say, 'we've decided what we want to do is go to Arkansas and work on a little farm. Ain't so good to be even half-way rich.' 'Oh, my God Almighty, children,' I'd tell them, 'you must be crazy. That's all there is to it. You must be crazy.' 'Course, my mother and daddy weren't crazy. Even without going to school much, they were good folks. I was about to say they were special folks, the most special, I suppose, I've ever had the good fortune to know."

Big Joe Winkler says he was born in Appalachia. He never mentions the name of a town, just Appalachia. That's all he says. He says he'll die in Appalachia, too, because he'll never move away. "Nothing to move to," he says. "Nothing to move back to, neither. My spirit's here. My name is here. Whole country could float away and just leave me this land and I'd be happy. I'd be happy. Just have a little bit to eat and folks around here who know me like they do." His eyes brighten and he looks like he might want to grin. " 'Course, I might need a little financial credit now and again, jobs being what they are and chances being what they are for a man my age, and size, and good old-fashioned intelligence. What do you say to *that*?"

Fifty-three-year-old Joe Winkler used to work for a mining company in West Virginia. An accident in which his left leg was crushed ended that job, but he was lucky because a coal company quickly employed him as a cook in one of their large kitchens. Joe Winkler told them he didn't know soup from soap, but a man named Harry Hedrow, a squat man with drooping eyes, told him he better take the job because they were scarce as hell, and he better learn the difference between soap and soup damned quick if he expected to keep the job.

"So I took it," Joe Winkler says, gazing at the sky so intensely one might think he could see himself thirty years ago somewhere up in the mist. "And I learned how to dish out soup and all that slop they fed their employees there. Wouldn't touch the stuff myself," he laughs. "All right to poison folks you don't know, even some of your friends now and again, but only a fool poisons himself. Either a fool or a man who can't find in all the searching of his mind a single reason to stay alive. And that's a poor man, poorest man I'd say, because there's got to be something worthwhile that keeps a man alive. Lord didn't give you so much time on the earth that it does you or anybody else any good to shorten the time any. It all goes quick enough. I've made it through fifty-three years. Watched my hair change color four times. Imagine me being a boy with red hair, curls too. No one knew where they came from. Must have been a little bit of the Irish in me. Then it got blond. Had a woman tell me once, not long ago, she remembered when she was little seeing me with my blond hair. Didn't think I was all that bad, little tall for my age, she said. Said she was frightened, she remembered, by such a tall little fellow. I told her, tall ones like me never hurt no one. We're the ones who do the protecting, you know what I mean. Well then, my hair soon after got brown, then gray.

"They say your hair gets gray from worrying and sadness. I suppose that could be a pretty true statement. Never have known much luxury. Lost my wife when she was too young, from a sickness that never would have killed no city person. Never had doctors out here, though, or ones we could get to soon enough when we needed them. Twenty years, thirty years ago it wasn't any worse or better than what you see we got right now. Wife would get sick, it'd take you a couple of days before the doctor would come. Cars were always breaking down. So few folks had them to begin with, and the ones they had weren't any good in the first place. Then maybe the doctor would come and he'd say, 'This is the medicine for Bess.' And I'd stand there like a fool looking at the man because I knew it'd be a lot more days 'til I got what he wanted me to get for her. He knew it too. Times like those, when you know it's going to be maybe a week between the time your wife gets sick and the time you're going to give her the medicine she should have been taking the day she got sick, you're looking into the eyes of that other fellow; or like the time that Harry Hedrow told me I should take the cook's job, times like those everybody's looking at each other and wondering, now what in the name of the good Lord are we doing living in this part of the world. What are we doing here, when no one has the troubles we got just to earn a living and take care of a wife.

"She wasn't anywhere near that sick that one time. She recovered, late as I was with the medicine, which I never did pay for, but she got a weakness in her body that never did go away. It stayed with her two more years 'til she died. Twenty-six years old and she was dead. Still have the bed she died in. Still sleep with the blankets that she sweated up so bad, and I'll tell you, the weather wasn't all that cold either. Fact is, I was sleeping in a chair no more than ten feet away and I didn't need a blanket. But the fever put her away in her sleep and there was nothing else to do but bury her myself. I remember how I felt a chill that night, sleeping like I was, in that chair. Woke up suddenly and looked at her like I *knew* she was dead. But she wasn't. Did the same thing for weeks. Pop up in bed and think, oh my good Lord, I just know she's gone.

But she never was. Sometime, she'd feel me doing it, too.
Weak as she was she'd sort of barely open an eye at me and say, 'Go back to sleep, Winkler, I'm still here.' She could hardly talk, she was so weak, but she was worried about me just like I was about her.

"I don't know, maybe we'd been better living somewhere with a lot of other people around. Maybe that would have made a difference. But you set up your home, you do the best you can, even where we were, knowing you're going to barely survive, and you stay by it, even when your partner gets sick, so sick she just ain't going to make it. You set up home like everybody else in this country sets up home, and that's where you stay. Big home, small home, one room with a two-holer out back. That's what you got, well then, that's what you got. She believed it too. I told her I'd move her but she said, no, she was staying in our house, not that you could really call it a house. But we called it a house. Wasn't after she died.

"Buried her myself. Never told no one. Now that's sort of different, I think, than most folks would have gone about it. I thought it over and I decided, she's my wife; I want this whole, what you might call an experience, with myself. So I dug a grave on a spot I thought was right. Naturally I had to go pick the rockiest soil North Carolina ever knew it had, but I went ahead and dug it. Then I made a sort of coffin for her, nothing special, worn-out pine, looked old, weathered, wood was checked, but it still had the smell you want to find with pine, and I put some of her things in it, and I buried her. Kept lots of her belongings so as to remind myself every day of what she had, what she was. Sort of pretended, too, that she was still around. Not that she'd come in the front door one day, only that she was still around, you might say. I knew after I buried her that morning I'd never marry again, never have a family. We was going to have a child, but we lost it before it got born. So I knew I was going to be alone from then on. I cried too. Like a baby. Many, many days after I buried her. Knew too I'd never leave the old house neither. It was close to what I'd always known, close to my wife too.

"Guess you could say that's my story. I sort of belong around here. That's why I say I'll never leave. Think a lot about when I die, being buried up there near my wife. That'd make me a part of the land all right, wouldn't it. Come out of the land, end up right back in it. Isn't that what they say? Then they'd have to say I was pretty darn loyal to this part of the country. But I always figure, who's going to know to bury me. There's nobody going to wake up at night checking on whether I'm still breathing, no one going to put me up there when I go. So I figure, I'll just rot away inside here and somehow what I was, and what my wife was too, will find its way back into the earth. So it all works out pretty nice at that, don't it?"

arly in her life Fanny Bruckner decided that whatever happened, her children would learn to play an instrument and receive an education everyone would agree as being the best money could buy. Solomon Rothstein, the man she married when she was nineteen, supported his wife's pledges. In addition, he resolved that if the Rothstein children selected law or medicine as a career, he would make the money available despite the fact that at the time, his own accountant business yielded barely enough money for himself and his wife. On June 18, 1944, the first of their two children was born. Martin Benjamin Rothstein was a healthy baby weighing just over seven pounds, and with hands, his parents agreed, of a surgeon; certainly not of an accountant. Definitely not a business man; possibly a lawyer. Maybe a dentist.

"How many times they told me this," Marty Rothstein, a psychiatrist finishing his residency training, recounted for me one afternoon at the Municipal Hospital. Removing his small black appointment book, he threw his white medical jacket over a chair, then inserted the book in the breast pocket of his suit coat. Putting his hands up for me to examine, he appeared like a small child eager to prove to his parents that he had just washed them. "Here, take a look at my surgeon's hands. The doctor part, I guess, they got right; the surgeon part, well, maybe I let them down a little."

"Being a psychiatrist's not so bad," I replied.

"To me or to you. To them, it's still a little confusing. They weren't formally educated so they don't know what psychiatry really means. My mother's right out of that old joke. She keeps telling me I'm a psychiatrist because I can't stand the sight of blood. 'Maybe you'll still change' is her favorite line. I've been on the couch two years already and that's all I talk about. I think I'm convinced somewhere in my head that I do have to change. It's like I have this primitive sense that psychiatry's illicit, and that maybe it is because I can't stand blood. My own personal Sophie Portnoy, what does she want from me?" He grinned. "You read the book?"

"Of course."

"What do mothers want? I went to an Ivy League college, an Ivy League medical school. I studied the piano eight years. What does it take to make your mother happy?"

"A private practice," I suggested.

"Look at this," he said, sitting in his leather desk chair and motioning me to take a seat opposite him on the couch. "You and my mother. It's a goddamn conspiracy. I see my first private patient tomorrow at nine o'clock and already I've got you siding with my mother against psychiatry."

"Chalk it up to transference." I kidded him.

"You know, that's a very sound idea. I will." We laughed.

After completing the handsome education his parents had wanted for him, Martin Rothstein, a tall bearded man with deeply set, dark brown eyes began a three-year residency program in psychiatry. As medical school wore on, the decision of whether to enter internal medicine, pediatrics, neurology, or psychiatry had become more and more perplexing to him. At the beginning of the fourth year he chose psychiatry, in a sense falling back on his college interests. As an undergraduate he had concentrated in psychology and literature, debating as late as his junior year whether, in the long run, medicine was as rewarding as graduate school. His parents and uncle openly pushed for medical school, while the woman with whom he was in love believed surgeons to be butchers and psychiatrists, capitalist fakes. She counseled him to be a poet, journalist, writer, or editor. His decision to enter medical school was finally settled through the advice of a friend. Jonathan Spiegelberg, a young pediatrician, convinced him that one can always write poetry but one can't simply decide to do a little surgery here and there.

The treatment of students and patients during his medical education encouraged Martin to pursue a career in psychiatry. "It just seemed," he told me, "that psychiatrists would be more thoughtful, more humane. They weren't, of course," he smiled, "but one clings to any ideology or dream in medical school because the curriculum is so medieval. The only thing that was really special about psychiatry was that there were so many Jews. It was like this little housing project there in the middle of the hospital. But with a name like Rothstein, where should I have gone? Orthopedics? Ob-Gyn? Maybe. I'd rather look down from the other end."

His thought prompted me to inquire about sexism in medical school.

"Sexism," he reflected. "Doctors and nurses. Nothing changes from childhood. We were horrible pigs, but you didn't think. Psychiatric training, internships, and I still saw women doctors as oddities. It's not a comfortable confession, though it lessens a little bit with time. Thank God college and medical school don't kill a person's capacity to learn. But sure, I was schooled in the idea that men were doctors and women were nurses who fawned over you and did everything they could to make your life bearable and easy. It's a laugh. Bearable and easy and you make eighty-thousand dollars a year and they make, like, $128.50 a week and would love to marry you. It's unbelievable." He had put his feet up on the Danish modern desk his wife and he had selected especially for the office. "My first major deduction," he had told me when I met him some four months before, as the days of his residency came to a close.

"Sexism reminds me," he broke into my thoughts, "of a fantastic dream I had last night. Tomorrow I see my first private patient, like I told you."

"Right on this couch, eh?" I patted the rough fabric.

"Right where you're sitting is where a man will be sitting tomorrow. There's going to be a man there calling me doctor and needing from me everything that that means. I'm going to cure him, is what he's thinking. I'm going to make it all good like his mother or father never did."

"You going to have your feet up on the desk?" I grinned at him, knowing his answer.

"Listen, man, I'm going to be so nervous I'll be lucky if I'm not sucking my thumb. Feet on the desk? They'll be on the floor, legs crossed, tie tied, coat buttoned. I even thought of shaving my beard tonight. Anyway, last night I had this dream that the patient comes in—notice I say patient—we don't see people, we see patients—and it's a woman. Not Mr., you know, X, whom I'm really going to be seeing, but a woman. You want to know her name?"

"Anna Freud?" I guessed.

"Leacock."

"I don't get it."

"Well, the last part you get." I nodded yes. "And Lea just happens to be by pure chance the name of the first girl I ever went out with. But you're not supposed to think I need analysis or anything," he joked. "I mean, when I finish with the past, I finish with the past."

"Yeah, me too," I said with a straight face.

"All right, so Miss Leacock comes in and sits down, right there," he pointed to the couch, "and I present myself as the polite, intelligent shrink. She looks up at the diplomas, you know, and I look up too, and we nod. Yes, Miss Leacock, I'm telling her with my eyes, I'm a trained psychiatrist ready and

waiting to help you. So she begins by telling me she's divorc-
ing her husband because she's having an affair, and she never
loved him anyhow, and she doesn't care now what happens to
their son—my wife and I have a son, in case I didn't tell you—
and I start to laugh. It doesn't seem to bother her, but I'm sitting in the chair laughing. Out loud. Then she says she's thinking of killing herself, and now I become really hysterical."

"That's a good word."

"A great one. I'm convulsed on the floor with the tears roll-
ing down my face, and she's talking about taking her life. Is
that a dream?"

"Marty, would you give me permission to write about this?"

"The dream? Yeah, I suppose so." He was suddenly serious
and thoughtful. "It's revealing, though I'm not concerned only about my own identity since nobody will know that. But
if you use it, you have to add the interpretation. You have to
say that it's not exactly what it seems. First of all, it's a dream
of great anxiety. There's a doubting of confidence, there's a
fear of what women, I suppose, will tell me, and not just out-
and-out sexist perversions. I suppose it shows that one's prior
life is very much a part of the therapy process." For the moment the two of us sat in silence.

Surely there is a power in the therapeutic relationship, I
mused, an inequality between the participants. The arrangement of furniture in a doctor's office, the patient's chair and
the doctor's chair, the angle at which they are set, symbolize
this asymmetry. Perhaps it works to become a valuable aspect
of the encounter, like the payment for services becomes a valuable part of the relationship. Maybe people do doubt a service when they get it for nothing. Maybe they are relieved to
unleash a certain core of emotions along with money. But
now, in this instant, the power was here on the couch with
me, for I felt Marty trying to cover over the vulnerabilities he
had just revealed. We confess to journalists, psychiatrists, min-
isters, teachers, and parents, but once the words are said, it
doesn't always feel quite the way it is supposed to, no matter
how much the other person says we are stronger and purer
for it.

"I don't need to include dreams," I said. "I just thought
this one was important."

"No, it's not that. If the psychiatrist has no touch with his
feelings, outside of his own therapy, naturally, it's no good.
That's surely the creative part, the creative—what should I call

it—the creative energy of the therapeutic exchange. If it's only you, the patient, pouring out this stuff, then it's no good.
But this is the connection, you see, with writing, with art
generally, I imagine. Just to have the feelings is not enough.
I'm not casting aspersions on some of psychiatry's modern
competitors. But the expression of feelings, you see, can be
incomplete. It's like a dream. So the feelings are there. Images are there too. Anxiety, fright, primitive kinds of sensa-
tions are all over the place. Lea Bentner, that first girl, I have
one thought about her: how terrible I was. How frightened I
was. How sexually immature I was. In reality, if anyone should
laugh, it's her. It was a sad, lost time of my life which I bring
back now and then in therapy, but you hurt people on the
way. You hurt them in many ways." He paused. "Let me finish this other thought.

"I was telling you about feelings and their connection to
art." His tone was modest as he hunted for these complex notions. "The connection for me is in control. Not even the conscious understanding of feelings, but control. The putting
into action, into everyday life, of these feelings so that they
benefit you. They must raise you somehow. See what I'm saying? If it's totally based on understanding, if everything is
understood and analyzed, you stop listening, to everybody,
especially yourself. Then you're the dogmatic doctor who nobody needs, except the A.M.A." He was not joking. His face
showed lines of belligerence, or was it regret. "I think if there
are therapeutic goals, one of them must be to have a certain
control over oneself. This leaves room for intuition. It's the
I-don't-know-why-I-said-that phenomenon. But expression of
feelings isn't enough; dreaming isn't enough, primary process
isn't enough. It has to be disciplined, not controlled like a
prison controls, but in the way that the ego is the executive,
as the man said. Anyway, that's one dream. Now let me tell
you a daydream that I had this morning so you shouldn't
think I'm trying to hide that dream with a lot of academic
talk."

"I didn't think you were."

"You probably did a little. You do therapy."

"I thought that a little."

"You know, people ask, what are psychiatrists? Their kids
are neurotic, they're rich, they're prone to suicide. It's so
damn hard to talk about what shrinks are."

I reminded Marty that my purpose in talking with him was

to explore the way his own life as a young psychiatrist, just
this week, commencing private practice, was going.

"But people generalize," he protested mildly.

"Yes, people generalize."

"You write a piece about one psychiatrist, people will read
into it *all* psychiatrists."

"They may. But look," I replied. "You examine a patient
and say paranoid schizophrenia. You diagnose, I diagnose."

"But we don't generalize," he came back.

"At times we do. We speak about *mental* patients, *all* the
paranoids, *all* the psychopaths. . . ."

"I suppose."

"So maybe," I suggested, "someone might read this and
say, this is a human being, with courage, with intelligence
and sensitivity, who does good work and who also makes mistakes . . ."

"God forbid," he grinned.

" . . . who has impulses and desires. You want people to
think you're not human?"

He hesitated before answering. "You want the truth?"

"You'd like to be a bit above human. A step, right? Not a
big one, but a step."

"Why not a big one?" He smiled at me kindly. "Why can't
I buy into the doctor myth a little too? Eight years since college. Since *college*, my friend. I don't really like speaking this
way because there's a lot of mythology and adoration connected with being a doctor. But there's a lot of crap too you
have to take, and when the guy in the pharmacy calls you 'doc'
it feels very good." He leaned back in his chair as though he
had said his piece. "Yes, I suppose I want some of that special
treatment. I confess to feeling that I've earned it."

"Which means the money too?" I asked, with some bitterness which he detected.

"Hey, you can't resent me for that. Not with the salaries
I've been making for the last ten years. Jesus, I was at the poverty level when I was working twelve to fifteen hours a day.
Yeah, I want some of the money. Other guys are making it.
I'm almost twenty-nine. I went to college with guys who are
lawyers now, or in business, who are making thirty grand a
year, and more, while I'm on a fellowship stipend which pays
less than thirteen thousand. So I want it, yes."

Marty Rothstein leaned toward me, rested his elbows on
his knees, and glanced quickly at the door. "I had a patient

about three weeks ago who was telling me about his anger toward, I guess it was a surgeon that he owed money to. What he was saying reminded him that he owed the hospital for something else too. He was ranting on about this and I was doing my best to understand, appear sympathetic, you know. But inside I was thinking, I'm glad you're not going to be a regular patient of mine because if you owed me money I might refuse to see you. I swear to God, that's what I was thinking. If you don't pay me, I may not see you. If we agreed on a price, you come up with the money or I don't have to stay with you. You can see someone in the clinic."

"Does that thought frighten you?" I asked.

He thought about the question for a moment. "Yes and no. It bothers me that I might tune out for a while during therapy, which everyone does, but about the money situation, no. You make an agreement to pay, you pay. You pushing for something more important?"

"I am."

"Well, let's do it then. The issue, I think, that confronts every psychiatrist, psychologist too," he looked over at me, "is private practice versus—what do you want to call it—public service, maybe, clinic work, teaching, that kind of thing. Lower paying stuff, all right?" He nodded his head. "There can't be anybody that makes it through any medical school and sees all the sickness you see who doesn't want to treat people. You walk on the street and see someone lying there, it's like an instinct to help them."

"Although some laws make that instinct tough," I interjected.

"That's a lot of crap. If you want to help, you can help. You don't have to be afraid. Anyway, I think Tom Dooley thoughts, and Schweitzer thoughts. I think community clinics, I think hours working for the poor. But I know what's going to happen."

"You're going to end up in private practice."

"I'm going to end up in private practice," he repeated softly. "Right now that's the way I want it. I might have been more political when I was young, but it's like you get sucked into a style of life, and money and cars and homes and all the rest are part of it. What can I say? I'll give time here and there, teach residents probably, but I'll end up with most of my time devoted to private practice. Even if I work in a hospital part time, five, ten, twenty hours a week, that's just another

adjunct to private practice. You think these big-shot psychiatrists working in hospitals see poor people in clinics? You're
crazy. Very few doctors do. I'm not dumping on psychiatry
only. It's the entire practice of medicine. I see it, you see it,
we're all part of it. Some good-looking woman walks into the
clinic who goes to college and the interns and residents fight
for her. Some smelly little Negro kid comes in and everybody
shoves him off on a social worker or medical student or mental health worker. Who's kidding who? There are a few dedicated people who want to effect change somehow both in the
profession and in the society, but the rest of us talk. I'm a
talker. I don't want to go in the ghetto and see knife wounds
and people blabbering from neurological problems and paranoid schiz's. I could very well lie to you, you know, and pass
off some kind of gorgeous idealism which I probably would
if this were some newspaper promotional stuff. But what the
hell, it's better to have the truth even if no one knows who
the guy is who's telling it. Maybe it's just easier. Maybe, like
it happens to some people, you change when you're forty.
What's the name of the guy who operates the Mather Clinic
in Piedmont?"

"You mean Gerard Pressman?"

"Right, Gerry Pressman. There are lots of guys like him
who after ten, fifteen years of private practice want to get
out and see the rest of the world. So that happens." He let
out a long breath. "But for now I'm part of the arrangement
that says the more money you have, the more likely the
chance of seeing a psychiatrist privately in his office. I guess
for a while I want to be the psychiatrist in that office."

"Do you get pressured on this?" I asked.

"No, not really. This profession's probably no different
than yours. If you gripe and complain and protest and make
a lot of noise, *that* passes as political action for a lot of people. But it's a lot of crap. You still treat the rich differently
than the poor, at least most of us do."

"You ever read Rieff's *The Triumph of the Therapeutic*?"

"No, should I?"

"I think so."

"Like Szasz? There's an enormous amount I should read,"
he replied almost penitently.

"You and me both."

I wanted the sudden tension to be gone. In response to his
words I thought of those occasions when doctors mention

their patients by name and of those occasions when they ada-
mantly refuse to. This was an honest, forthright man sitting
silently now, in front of me, someone totally aware that his
confessions would not dissipate medical and social problems
one iota. I'm not a savior or crusader or anything else that's
special, except that I'm a doctor, is what in effect he had told
me. A doctor, which means a lot of good things; a doctor,
which means narcissism, materialism, power, and manipula-
tive things too. I'm proud and I'm not proud, though I'm also
not ashamed, is what he had told me.

Dr. Marty Rothstein breathed heavily as he fished for something in the pocket of his suit jacket. This was only our second
meeting in this office. Previously, we had met in his downstairs office with the heating pipes on the ceiling making an
infuriating racket and a bookcase hiding the main drain for
the upstairs floors. Once, when the flushing sound had made it
impossible for us to hear one another, he joked about how
the office traditionally causes everyone to think anal. "What
the hell," he had said, "it's the stage of life I handle best. So,
people come here with sexual problems, phobias, ticks, they
hear the flushing and the pipes up there clanging with the de-
mons inside, and they switch over to anal problems. Before
they leave I give them a copy of Philip Slater's book and they
feel better."

"America and the invention of the flush toilet," I had muttered, reminded of Slater's amazingly insightful book.

"The guy's brilliant," Marty had said. "He must have been
shrunk." He was only half joking. The flushing incongruities
of that first office had annoyed him. Ironically, it prompted
discussions of his supervision with two outstanding psychiatrists, one of whom was a psychoanalyst as well. "I'm tied to
them, right up to here." He had made a gesture as though slit-
ting his face in half. "I need them though. I learn from them,
especially Pincus. He's brilliant. Sometimes, you know, you'd
like to parade the John Pincuses of the world before the public and say, you all think psychiatry's easy and there's nothing to learn; listen to this man. He's young too. Middle forties,
but he's brilliant. He cures people. I'm so nervous with him
that most of the time I forget everything I'm supposed to tell
him about my work. It's like a defense mechanism. In the mornings when I'm going to see him I make a list in my mind of
what I'm going to tell him. Then I hit his office and it's gone.
It's like I can feel my memory closing on me. I can actually see

gates blocking my thoughts. Sometimes I lie. It's like I'm trying to present myself as Freud, but on a very, very bad day.
It's like Pincus should know I'm brilliant, so if I goof it will
be all right. Once in therapy, about six months ago, I suddenly
got two patients confused. I mean, I knew who I was talking
to, but I had his relatives confused with the names of another
patient's relatives. Three times I misnamed them. Once with
his mother, once with his brother, and once with the name of
the girl he goes with." Marty had held up three fingers. His
face had had an excited, 'it's all true' look on it. "You know
what the guy said to me? 'I think you're a fine doctor, Dr.
Rothstein, but I think your watch is an hour fast!' "

I had exploded with laughter and as I did, the flushing
sound began anew, and the two of us roared in the lugubrious
basement office of an important urban hospital, our own
sounds muffled by the noises of the pipes and the double door
leading to the dark corridor outside.

"You think I told Pincus about those slips? Not once." He
was still smiling. "I told my analyst though, which is itself significant because it means I was more concerned with how *I*
was faring than with how he was faring."

"Maybe you were wishing too," I had interjected, "that it
was the other patient? Were you bored with this one?"

Marty had nodded his head and smiled. "Out of my mind,"
he conceded. "I think my wish at that moment was to have
anybody else for a patient but this guy." He had watched for
a moment as I wrote in my notebook. "You finished?"

I nodded.

"All right, now take this down too because all of this stuff
is more complicated. I used to always get very tired seeing this
patient. Before I faced up to what it meant I just felt fatigue.
All right? Then I started putting some of it together in my
analysis. Pincus himself sent me this patient, which was why,
incidentally, I was in supervision with him."

"Did the patient know?"

"That's interesting too," Marty had smiled. "I never asked
Pincus. I didn't want to know. I think they call it dependen-
cy. Anyway, on the couch one morning right after all this
business with the names, I was talking about Pincus, who
turns out to have the same initials of the mother of a boy I
went to camp with when I was what, eleven, twelve, who I
competed with like you wouldn't believe. If he swam fifty
yards in however many seconds, I'd have to swim two seconds

faster. You can guess what symptom I used to have when I'd come home from that camp each summer."

"Fatigue?"

"Fatigue. Exactly. So this neurotic thing gets played out in therapy, and sadly, in someone else's therapy."

"So what's the implication?" I had asked as the phone rang.

"Doctor Rothstein," he answered. "Yes . . . yes . . . I did . . . I ordered valium for him and suggested the possibility of hospitalizing him too." He seemed disgruntled. "Two milligram tablets as often as he wants. Say, when in the hell are they going to pass a law to let psychologists give out drugs? . . . Yeah, I'll cover for him. . . . Peter, it's like 1984 with Kafka thrown in. . . . All right, I'll talk to him, put him on." He had put his hand over the phone and, peering down at the wastebasket, said to me, "Medicine, hospitals, psychiatry. If patients knew what was going on here, even in this place, they'd go to their grocers for therapy."

"You see the movie *Hospital*?" I asked.

As he nodded, the voice in his ear drew him away. "George, how are you?" he asked pleasantly, his body moving in the chair. His conversation, which I tried not to overhear, was obviously with a nonmedical therapist who had run up against the problem of not being able to prescribe drugs but who dreaded the humiliation and the threat to the patient's trust in him caused by the necessity to turn to a real doctor. Marty had concluded with the words, "Don't let those idiots castrate you, and call me when his depression lifts, or at least look for suicidal material then." Then he laughed in response to something the psychologist had said. "Yeah, so you got one left, who'll ever know?" He hung up still smiling. "Where was I?"

"That maybe residents are too young to do therapy," I reminded him.

"Sure they're too young. Let me ask you, should Ph.D. students have their dissertations published?"

"Some, I suppose," I had answered.

"Some, but as a regular practice?"

"I don't know. Probably not. But the profession pushes us to."

"Bingo! And how about teaching? Were you ready just 'cause you had your degree?"

"In terms of showmanship, yeah," I responded blithely. "Substantively I'm not there yet."

"It's the same with us," he said. "Of course we're not ready, but who's going to do it, and how is anybody going to start? When I think now of what I knew two years ago, two years," he almost shouted the words, "and I was doing thirty hours a week of treatment." He saw my surprise. "That's right. Thirty hours. And what I knew at the end of my first year as a resident you could put in a thimble."

"The patients don't know," I had said quietly.

"They don't know, and because the bulk of the ones I saw were poor and uneducated and had nobody in their communities to talk to, they didn't care. 'Mrs. Lopez, I'm Dr. Rothstein,' " he announced himself to an invisible woman, and then made a sort of spitting sound with his mouth. "That's all they needed to learn. They were in the hands of a doctor. College students too. They didn't care. They *did* care what you said though." He had stared at me. "Then there's the other side. If residents with medical training don't do therapy, and the medical profession remains as isolated and smug as it has, you end up turning therapy over to anybody who wants to hang up a shingle. *That* I'm not for. They don't all have to go to medical school, but I sure wish there could be something that everyone would have to do to qualify to do therapy."

"How about demanding knowledge of the Bible?"

"The Bible?" he questioned me incredulously.

"Sure."

"I suppose it's as good as anything," he said after contemplating the idea for a moment. "The Old Testament," he grinned. "God, what would it be like to have doctors who are really educated. What an incredible thing to have the power we have and the status and have people feeling that we're wise, particularly in psychiatry, and walk around not ever having heard of half the books that people on the subways are reading. Not only that, but such fundamental issues go unchallenged, or, you know, they're left up in the air. Who's really sick? What determines whether I, with training, with a year or two or three of experience, decide if someone's sick and needs to go to a hospital? Here's a confession you can use in your story. On appearance alone, I'm already deciding the fate of a patient. Whether or not they're attractive, man or woman, somehow goes into that calculation. So how do you deal with that in psychiatry, doctor? How do you deal with a desire to have a black patient or two just so no one will accuse you of anything, or so you don't have to feel you're furthering a profession which has its racist side too?" He was nodding in his characteristic way, a way I might like to call rabbinical; nodding as if to say how well I know all this from my experiences on this earth.

My discussions with Dr. Martin Rothstein continued at reasonably regular intervals well into the winter. It was now almost nine months since we had met, four months from the time he had officially completed his residency at the hospital and commenced private practice. His new office in a suite which he shared with two other psychiatrists was particularly handsome, a far cry from the basement cell with its flushing basso continuum, as we decided it should be designated.

Anticipating that within a couple of years he would enter a psychoanalytic institute for further training, he had selected an office model in which patients leaving do not see those waiting to be seen. All three doctors, furthermore, had staggered their schedules so that a patient would rarely see either of the other two doctors.

"You look very prosperous," I said, on visiting the new office for the first time one cold December afternoon.

"I don't feel it," he said. "Fact is, I still feel I'm playing doctor, especially since I still have supervision."

"You continue that, eh?"

"Little bit, sure. I'm not ready to be totally independent yet," he smiled. "I'll be up for that when I'm fifty."

"So how's private practice?" I asked, pulling out my notebook. We watched one another closely.

"You think," he began, "we should ever talk about some of the feelings between *us* that we always push aside?"

"Like what?"

"You know."

"I envy you, Marty," I admitted.

"Why? 'Cause of this?" he said, waving his hands about to encompass the surroundings.

"Sure. And other things."

"That I'm a doctor?"

"That too, I guess."

"Credentials don't make anybody unique. I envy you your work too."

"Being a doctor matters," I said. "I'm older than you and somehow your status always makes me feel you're as old or older."

"Maybe that's because I'm losing my hair faster than you."

I didn't say anything in response. "I suppose you're right. Being a doctor matters to me. I was thinking after seeing a patient the other day that I wasn't really so sure what he was talking about, what it meant in a therapeutic sense. And a part of me said, what do you care, you're a doctor and that probably matters to him as much as anything."

"I think there's truth in that," I said, "even with all the defensiveness."

"I guess there is. I just feel," he went on in a halting way, "that I'm not prepared for all this. I still feel that I'm in high school, driving my father's car, taking a girl out and wanting to impress the hell out of her with my father's money. My father's accountant money, as little as there was. That's really the sensation I have. It's not mine, and yet it feels very good. Too good. I'll bring a patient in here, you know, for the first time and they'll look around with admiration."

Marty and I took in the room together. There was the handsome desk and couch brought over from the hospital, two modern matched chairs, a small wall bookcase filled mainly with psychiatric texts and journals, and on the floor near the window several large schefflera plants. On the walls he and his wife had hung his diplomas and certificates, a water color painted by his former college roommate, a Paul Klee poster that for some reason made me think of Jung, and above the couch a Moroccan rug that enhanced the décor and kept the room quiet.

"It's nice in here, is what they have written on their faces," he continued. "I have to laugh 'cause I never see that expression, that way they check things out as a test of how successful I am, without thinking of the nights Paula and I in our ratty old clothes were plastering and painting in here. I must have made fifteen holes in that wall before we got that one rug to stay up. What I'd love to say to them is, you better believe it's nice and cheerful and rich here, and I work damned hard listening to you even if you think you over pay. So I do it for them and for me, and I take it very seriously."

"I'm impressed."

"Once in my life I'd like to be able to not be the humble, well-defended doctor. I'm really a very snotty guy, and I think that now that it's all behind me I probably want to live in a snotty way. I have my boards left to take, you know, comprehensive examinations in neurology and psychiatry, and I'll pass them with some work, although God only knows," he said shaking his head, "I can't remember a thing from neurology. All I think about is that when I get those results I'll probably raise my fees. Is that gross, you think?"

I shrugged my shoulders. "I don't know."

"You don't like that kind of talk."

"I think the same thoughts," I told him. "You confess by talking, I confess by writing. We both believe there's an automatic purification built in."

"I guess so," Marty responded pensively. "Anyway," he said, breaking the mood, "I made a note to tell you a few of my thoughts on the first hour. Mr. S., who I'd seen once or twice in the hospital, actually, was the first private patient, though he wasn't the first I saw in this office." I recalled the dream in which Marty laughed in the presence of a woman bleeding with depression. "As the guy was speaking, I suddenly had this thought that I could compute how much I was earning per minute. Then I could time him for a minute and do a word count and eventually get down to what I was earning for each word." I tried to remain expressionless. "You're thinking 'crass,'" Marty remarked. "Add to it that I realized that time passed much faster when I was talking than when he was talking. Which reminds me that you notice I've placed the clock where I can see it but the patients can't."

"That's tradition. Like a picture of Freud somewhere."

Marty laughed out loud. "Mine's at the framer. Tradition also says you're not supposed to have pictures of your wife and kids around."

"Yeah, I know," I muttered, "so patients can fantasize whether or not you're a eunuch."

"Which reminds me of the sexual fantasies." There was a strange urgency in his voice, as though this were to be our last meeting. Perhaps having seen the first private patients in his new office meant that a substantial part of his life was now permanently completed.

"I want you to know," he was saying sarcastically, "that I am wonderfully ecumenical in my sexual fantasies about patients. I fantasize about all of them. Male, female, young, old, I snoop and peer and heaven only knows what else. No one should think for a minute that this sleeping with your patients act is an impulse that only a few misbegotten souls entertain. It's in here, man," he proclaimed with intensity. Behind the desk I saw him reach for his groin. "The encounters in this room evoke your body and your mind, your past and your present no matter what neurotic complex you've resolved. The patient brings all his life to that moment, and you better bring all of yours. The difference is in control and discipline. But you bring it all. Private practice, clinical practice, you bring your guts and your genitals along with your mind. And your heart. The patient brings in his mother, you bring in your mother. You don't have to talk about her, but you better get her in there. Everybody they mention or describe reminds you of people. I used to try to get these people out of my mind until I realized one day the kind of insight a doctor can get from thinking about the people from his childhood and adolescence his patients make him think of. What they ought to make as a prerequisite for psychiatry is going to a huge public grammar school and high school so you can have millions of characters to be reminded of some day when you're sitting in that chair." We looked over at the brown leather swivel chair which everyone in the world would recognize as belonging to the doctor.

"The Bible too," I said, adding my own prerequisite.

"The Bible too," he nodded. "Both testaments."

Minutes later, our meeting ended and Marty escorted me to the small elevator outside the waiting room.

"You're ready to write, aren't you?" he asked.

"I think I'm going to try a draft. I'll show it to you."

"I'd like to have a look at your stuff, and me through your eyes."

"You can take out things if you have second thoughts."

"No, it's not that. That's not going to bother me," he said, somewhat perplexed. "It's—what I'd really like you to say in the article is that while I was willing to be interviewed, to kind of be—you know—like the patient, the difference is that *you* came to *me*. I wanted to say some things as a confession, I suppose, just to show the other side. But the compulsion wasn't mine. I was willing, obviously, but I didn't initiate it." He pointed his finger at me. "That's an important distinction."

We shook hands.

Outside in the street I thought first about him and tried to imagine the faces and voices of his patients. Was the woman just now entering the building "one of his"? Then there was my own career and history to think about, and my conflicts about doctors, although not psychiatrists especially. One wants to believe, I thought, that the mythology imputed to medical people might at last be ending and that the life-and-death powers with which they presumably deal are losing their mystery and awesomeness.

Yet, this was a special man, a man made special in part because of his training and status, or at least because of the joining of his being with the role our culture has evolved for him. They're just mortal, I whispered to myself in the cold. They're capable of the same dreadful misjudgments and remissions we all make. And because each is an individual, I shouldn't let myself aggregate "them." Psychiatrists. Still, when they're good, they're really quite special.

Part Four

Observations of Social Behavior

My research into men's consciousness raising groups began with an examination of publications I had never seen: *Body Politic*; *The Furies*; an article on rock in *Sabot*; Jack Sawyer writing in *Liberation* on the stereotypes of sex roles and the bondage these stereotypes create; Nick Benton, in *The Effeminist*, objecting to the word brother in the male liberation movement; an unknown author venting his anger toward women in *Chicago Seed*; Henry Balson claiming that while Norman Mailer "is in the end, oppressive in many ways to women and to himself, he struggles honestly with real problems that a man, particularly a neurotic Jewish male like himself, like myself, like Bernie Farber, faces in America."

My research began too, hunting in the *People's Yellow Pages* for the names of men who might allow me to look in on their groups. It began standing in front of a university bulletin board that displayed strips of colored paper notifying readers of group meetings, discussions, political planning sessions, requests by one man to meet with another; and above all these notices, the words "Homophile League." It began in front of that bulletin board, remembering myself as an adolescent, apart from girls, apart from men and women, tenuously connected to the boys, telling dirty jokes, wondering about girls, wondering if others saw me as "queer" in posture or language, wondering whether everything about my development was coming out all right. Strangely, I thought about my sister, and the times I felt her capable of doing things and feeling things that were closed to me. While I might have been saddened by these differences, which my local culture taught me to interpret as sibling rivalry or a necessary biproduct of sex role differentiation, I was taught that the differences between my sister and me were essential for the working of our family and for the destiny of an entire civilization. The payoff, it was promised, would be delivered when I reached manhood.

In writing about the processes of socialization, Max Weber and Emile Durkheim arrived at the same theoretical point of view that Freud had reached in his notions of identification and internalization. Children, these theorists wrote, not only assume the attitudes, values, and perspectives of their parents; the learning process supports children's belief that they have developed these attitudes and values on their own. Sex role based behavior, therefore, seems to each of us to be basic, logical, the natural evolution of women and men. Sex role differentiation is a bit like learning language, in that we naturally learn the language of our parents; who would think twice about this? And who, in my generation, would have thought anything other than that men are men; which means men are not women, they don't cry in defeat or in a sentimental movie, they don't scream deliriously at a hockey game, they don't kiss when greeting one another, they put their hand near their mouth when whispering to a male friend, they learn that homosexuality is something to fear, like impotence or venereal disease, and that they better perform well because a man without a successful job, a decent income, and a promising career is only half a man, a boy whose voice never changed. This is what we believed. These were the attitudes, styles, emotions that, consciously or unconsciously, we internalized and labeled appropriate, masculine, healthy. Even those of us whose experiences with other cultures and values put us in conflict with these male role stereotypes, in the end bought into the masculinity currency and derogated those other values. Masculinity was godliness; effeminacy, a curse of the devil.

No one can accurately describe an era or decade, or capture the mood of a country on any issue. Yet periodically, words and especially seductive phrases are born; and a few words, or family of words, seem to survive a while, and are gradually incorporated into the flow of a country's political and social movements. Such words as conscience, conscious, consciousness represent a family of ideas and forces whose relatives are political ideology, human bondage, war, liberation, personal recognition, revolution, exposure, surveillance. In Massachusetts alone, I was able to discover over one hundred references to men's consciousness raising groups. In letters and in phone calls the words conscience and consciousness were passed on gently, as men, some young, some no longer young, advised me of the need for men to become aware of the oppressive forces of institutions and the ways these forces are internalized through the learning of proper sex role behavior. "To raise a man's consciousness," a man from the western part of the state said, "we are seeking to make him conscious of the forces of evil. Not metaphysical forces, just plain old everyday forces of values that determine his life and make him fear feelings that are natural and beautiful. Poor dude walking around," this man went on, "afraid to embrace his close friend, afraid to fall in love with a man, afraid to love a woman if it means he can't go around telling his drinking buddies he's making it with every chick that comes along."

"You speak about personal things in your men's group?" I asked.

"Last night," he answered, "I told them that from time to time at my job at this store where I work, I have to excuse myself so I can masturbate. I told them what kinds of fantasies I conjure up and then they went ahead and shared their fantasies with me. You think you're up to that?" he challenged.

"I'm not sure," I replied.

"Well, you think about it, because it's doubtful we would let an outside observer come into the group anyway. The movement needs some publicity, but we've all seen how publicity can kill honest, human political movements. Our group feels you're either in all the way or you're not. The men's movement isn't set up for voyeurs and media freaks. We're not that hungry for new members anyway."

I heard similar sentiments elsewhere; namely, that while consciousness raising is a goal, exposure and intrusion must be carefully monitored, and the history of the particular group not disturbed. Soon several groups allowed me to attend sessions. I promised my new friends confidentiality even when they did not request it. As various reports indicated, the groups usually met at the home of one of the members, sometimes rotating from home to home. There was a bit of joking now and again about the presence of women, making certain a wife was out for the evening, and advising outsiders not to telephone during these special hours. Each group spoke of their feelings about my presence and purpose. No doubt I hid behind this outsider's role; no doubt too, these men recognized my hesitancy, and honored it.

"The biggest problem you normally run into in these sorts of groups," I was told after one session by a twenty-nine-year-old college professor, "is the old demon homosexuality. Put men together in a group and you arouse the panic. I remember when I first began I thought they'd make us get nude, or that all my homosexual fears were going to erupt and my whole life would break in two. You know what I mean? Go in one way and come out the other, as if men don't have both sets of impulses. But the result is I honestly think I'm a better human being, not just a better *man*, as the expression goes. I'm a better person."

An hour before in this group, which consisted of six men, seven including me, the topic of anger suddenly had surfaced.

"You're really angry with me, aren't you?" one man asked another.

"I'm not." The response was calm.

"You are!"

"What the hell gives *you* the wisdom to know what *I'm* feeling?"

"I can see it. I can hear it."

"Of course you can. *Now* I'm angry. You get me angry and then you say I'm angry. That's a helluva procedure."

"You were angry before," a third man says quietly.

"I'm getting angry at *your* quiet voice, I'll tell you."

"What's wrong with a quiet voice?" someone asked.

"Nothing, except that I doubt it's for real."

"Maybe you don't like it because quiet voices are supposed to belong to women."

"Oh my God, you guys are out of your minds. Quiet voices, women. My father had a quiet voice, so what's that got to do with anything?" Suddenly the man looked sheepishly at the others. We saw him pulling back, protecting himself until someone spoke.

"Hey, this is for you, for us, we're friends in here. This isn't an inquisition. If you want to tell us something, we'd like to hear it."

"My father," the man began slowly, "always used this quiet voice when he'd get angry with me. He could even hit us and not raise his voice. Oh, I just this second remembered what he used to tell me. 'Men,' he used to say, 'use their brains and their strength. A real man doesn't have to yell.' And I grew up believing that. I used to think Ernie Banks was a great man because he never yelled and Durocher wasn't a real man because he yelled at every call. Bald old Leo, and young handsome Ernie Banks."

"Ernie's getting bald too, now," someone added grinning.

"I never thought, I didn't think until this minute, how I connected silence with manliness. Is that what the hell they mean by the strong silent type!" The others laughed generously, communicating their support to this man. "I'm going out tomorrow morning and I'm going to yell. What do you think of that? Men can yell. If they can get themselves to cry, they can get themselves to yell."

I watched the others laughing and joking and heard their

expressions of how men must not fear emotions and deeply founded feelings. Several thoughts crossed my mind. I never had a brother, but as a child took a cousin and more recently a close friend to stand in for brothers. I fear crying as many fear vomiting or seeing someone who has been severely injured.

In another group, this one composed of seven grammar school and high school teachers originally brought together through their educational concerns, the discussion was centered on male and female fantasies. Early in this particular group's history, the men had engaged a professional encounter group leader. For a time they debated the merits of male and female leaders, recognizing that the sorts of "things" that happen with both are valuable. In the end, they chose a man, believing in the significance of an all men's group for their collective development. After a while, however, they asked the leader to leave. Their own private and career concerns, they told him, made him seem too much the outsider. Many groups report a similar history. Some still maintain leaders, but the majority I contacted were leaderless. Indeed, the concepts of leading, authority, and group facilitator had become the basis for many discussions on masculinity.

The fantasies in the teachers' group were balloons kept aloft by gentle pushes. The men spoke of what they imagined their male friends did on dates, of what sort of lives they imagined women teachers in their schools were having, and of their students:

"Jack Crawley right this minute is trying to get Marcia Cassidy to marry him." The men who knew these students laughed.

"Not exactly. He's trying to show her his manliness and she's getting interested." They laughed again. So far it sounded to me like any other men's group, a faculty lounge perhaps, a locker room. It sounded this way to the men as well.

"You guys," a thirty-two-year-old grammar school teacher began, "are just jealous of Mr. Crawley; his age, his face, his good looks, his strength, his success, as you describe it, with these girls."

"Aw, that's not so true," they protested.

"You guys," he persisted, "are avoiding working in here, right now."

"Since when do we have our noble leader back?" someone muttered.

"I'm not leading, Stan. I'm merely pointing out that that's

not what we do here. That talk's for school, until we can drum it out of there too. Don't you see? Masculinity, youth, the constant need we have to be young, virile studs. I mean, isn't that where we got going last time about feeling castrated being *male* teachers. You envy that kid, any kid, and you're buying one hundred percent the stereotype that every damn school in America continues to perpetuate. Any man who teaches has something wrong down here." He reached for his groin. The men were silent.

"I want to go back to last week." It was another man speaking now. The man next to me leaned over to say that the previous week they had been discussing Otto Rank's *Myth of the Birth of a Hero*. "I want to go back to hero worship and some things that have stayed with me. The hero in my life has always been bigger than me. He had to be strong and big. I always had this feeling that I would have to check him out too, when he's naked. Like I see Muhammed Ali ready to fight, or John Kennedy in his shorts running on the beach with his kids, or going sailing."

"You uncomfortable with your own body?" someone asked him.

"Don't you think the first hero is your father?" another inquired.

"Maybe, I don't know. I know that I want to depend on a strong man once in a while, and that this culture says you're not supposed to."

"Then *screw* the culture!"

"Yeah sure," he responded sarcastically. They were all talking at once.

"I want to lean on people, you know, depend on them and still have them think of me as being masculine."

"Why's masculinity so important to you?"

"Because you don't throw off your childhood that quickly, that's why. You don't go through the army and teach in schools and say that sex differences don't matter. I have male heroes. I have homosexual fantasies. I experience jealousy toward the boys in my class. I have nothing in the world in common with that group of principals and assistant principals, and I have a thing about seeing men who I think are good looking. I mean, really good looking."

"So do I," someone opposite him reported.

"I feel competitive with them; I feel intimidated by them."

"Keep going," another person encouraged him.

"I've said it all. I cannot freely love a man or a woman, and day in and day out I'm forced to pass myself off as this sensitive, gentle, genteel for that matter, man, not a woman, and everyday I hear students talking about this person or that person and you guys know damn well their criticisms are always the same: bad women are tough and bad men are effeminate."

"Emasculated."

"Queer."

"Tender."

"Gentle."

"Well, you guys are different, but so far the comfort and freedom I probably feel here, even in front of a stranger," he glanced at me without expression, "isn't enough apparently when I try to carry it over to, you know, people and places outside of here."

For the moment no one spoke. I looked at the others who were concentrating on the man who had spoken. He found it difficult to be watched, even in this caring way.

"Let's not stare him out of here," someone advised.

"I'm not trying to do that. I'm sorry, Steve, if you thought I was staring at you in that way."

"I didn't feel that."

"I only wanted to tell you that I, well, that I love you as much as I can knowing you a little in here and a little at school, and that I think you must be a good teacher. You're someone I would entrust my own kids to, and someday I hope I have some to entrust to you. I suppose that in a way, since I'm new at this thing, that you're kind of a hero to me."

The others seemed pleased. Steve was touched by these words.

"I don't even have to strip to the waist for you?" he asked smiling.

"You already have," came the reply.

As they spoke, touched each other on the hands and arms, and as those in chairs pulled closer to the men sitting on the floor, two thoughts crossed my mind. The first thought was of a man in the Roxbury district of Boston, a poor black man whose last three jobs have ended abruptly because of industrial and governmental cutbacks. Sipping gin, one afternoon in a bar, this forty-eight-year-old man said, "And now you take a good look at me, young man that you are. Look at me and see failure. Not just unemployed, not just scrapping after dollars in the streets, but a failed man. There isn't a woman nowhere in the world who can feel failure as a man feels it, and I feel it. In here." He spread his fingers over his chest. "All those years I was growing up they taught me that a man brings in money for his family, and that's what I did. Quit school in the fourth grade and went to work. Been working since then until right now. But if you don't work, if you want to work and you can't work, then they might just as well be killing you. That's the long and the short of it. They might just as well be killing you. They're saying to me you ain't a man no more. Ain't exactly sure what you are, but you ain't no man. Right now I guess I'd have to agree with them. When I worked at the factory in Watertown I was a man, earning my money like a man, competing head to head with the man next to me and the man above me. But that's all finished now. Maybe though, 'cause I'm not young anymore, I don't feel so terrible about it, 'cause it wasn't my doing. It's *his* doing, the man in Washington. He's the one makes it so's that none of these men in this bar are real men. They're half men, beat up animals ready for the heap somewhere.

"But you want to know what makes me saddest of all is that I ain't got a single individual anywhere in this world that I can drink with and talk to. Not a one. Not a black one, not a white one. Can't talk to my sons, they'd write me off. Ain't got a father since twenty-five years. Don't go to church. Don't have no best friend. Had one, but he's gone. Take it into my mind every once in a while to get myself sick from alcohol, real sick, lying face down on the street sick, so's they could put me in a hospital and I could talk to the doctor." He looked down at his drink and sighed. "Yessir. If a person wanted to do me a favor, he'd go outside that door now and find me a brother, a real brother. Someone I could talk to, talk men things to, someone to give me a second, third, fourth, fifth chance. Every man needs a brother, you know. Even you, my white brother."

The second thought was but a brief recollection. I am in the first grade. A new boy stands in the doorway dressed in a tiny suit and tie. He appears confident, someone who will be popular among classmates. I recall a shudder of fright, jealousy, competition, a sensation of being threatened. That is the entire image. I never see the boy take a step; he merely stands at the threshold. I will have this tense new boy experience again and again as I grow up, and nothing like it will ever involve women.

In a third group I met seven new men, some of whom knew one another before an official men's group was inaugurated. There had never been a leader in this group, although they experimented with the notion of having rotating leaders who would take responsibility for the meeting place, finding pertinent literature, and running the actual meeting. Settling on the idea of a collective, they discarded this plan.

Two members of this group were practicing homosexuals, two were married, another lived with a woman, another had confessed to having had only one experience with a woman. Two of the men, I was advised, were "genuine delinquents once upon a time," one of them having served in prison for robbery. All were between twenty-three and twenty-eight. As a sort of initiation they asked me to recount two personal experiences, one that revealed the sexist side of me, and one when I felt imprisoned by my masculinity. For the former request I told them how I tried to "masculinize" a woman professor in college. For the latter, I confessed my ambitions and how I accounted for failure. I told them too, of a fantasy I share with several friends, of writing a best-selling (and critically acclaimed, naturally) book and walking into a party, late, and having women swoon over my, well, everything. The men looked at one another and nodded. I had passed. They warned me of the need for confidentiality and the dangers of bad press.

The meeting began slowly. They believed my presence was an impediment. They spoke briefly of prisoners of war, Nixon, and the "nonhumanity that lived in his every breath." They considered the possibility of organizing men's groups at a local military installation. Someone referred to psychological studies conducted on bomber crews. Grinker and Spiegel's *Men Under Stress* was mentioned. They spoke about the women's movement and an eloquent article by Warren Farell. "Hey, when you write the piece," one of the men squeezed my arm, "don't psychoanalyze us. I mean, don't do a number: he's twenty-five and he grew up in New York and he began hating his father when he was four and he was toilet trained at twelve. You know what I mean?"

"When *were* you toilet trained, Peter?" someone asked. Everyone laughed.

"Last week. In here." Their laughter subsided.

"Yeah?"

"Yes, actually, when I finally got it off my chest about my wife."

The week before Peter had recalled a dream in which his wife was unfaithful to him. In the dream he hunts for the man but each time he is about to catch them together, the man disappears. In the end, after an inexplicable interval in which he plays little league baseball with a group of lepers, an interval which had the others convulsed until they faced the imagery of mutilation, castration, and punishment, he discovers his wife's lovers to be his brothers in the group.

"I loved you guys then," Peter explained.

"Why?"

" 'Cause it turned out that you loved what I loved."

"Bullshit! You hated the group for getting between you and your wife."

"I don't think so."

"Sure you did. It's her against us and you felt you couldn't have us both."

"I *want* both."

"Exactly," several of the men cried out in unison.

"Peter, why can't you let yourself go in here? I think you think intimate discussions have to breed intimate relations." Peter protested.

"No, really, I think that's right. Maybe your marriage is fine and good, and sex is terrific, but in here you don't let go."

"You think?"

"I'm pretty sure."

"Maybe it's them." Peter pointed to the two who had confessed their homosexuality.

"What is it about them?" someone wondered.

Peter seemed confused. "It's that—look, I'm pushing thirty, my job prospects are rather predictable at this point. You know, community politics, a little teaching, a lot of hustling. I've been married eight years, we don't have kids, it's getting a little boring. She's in her women's group, I'm in my men's group, I suppose I think the next step is to become a homosexual or something. I don't know, maybe I want to. I've never had anything that even resembles that kind of experience. I've never been picked up, I've never approached anyone, although you know, every once in a while when I'm talking with a man, I'll find myself studying the line of his beard, where it ends, you know, and the skin is very smooth." He felt his cheek. "Then I'll have this sudden urge to kiss the guy. Not like those idiots on television. Just a little kiss. Then I'll think, Jesus Christ, you don't need a *men's* group, man, you need a *therapy* group."

No one spoke.

"I'm really sorry that you think of yourself as needing therapy," one of the others said at last.

"Well, maybe that's extreme," Peter admitted. "Maybe I need an affair. Maybe I'm a pig. Maybe I'm angry with my wife for not needing me and feeling that I've never been able to just say that right out to you, or her, or anyone."

"You think she's going to leave you?" someone asked delicately.

"She may," he responded in a matter-of-fact way. "She may very well leave me." He was biting his lip, and looking down.

"You want to split from her?"

"No, I don't at all. I'd like kids. I'd like, if you'll forgive me, a nice marriage. Truthfully, I guess I want the kind of marriage you're not supposed to want anymore. I'd also like a noncompetition-have-to-be-a-strong-man-every-minute kind of work situation."

No one commented on Peter's words. They were looking away from him. Peter was crying.

"It's just so damn hard to keep this goddamn posture of manliness, this strength you're supposed to have all the time, this getting things done efficiently, planning for the future, fearing that you might fail or that you're not as good as someone or maybe much better than someone, or that you're not getting the rewards. I don't understand sometimes why women want *anything* we have. I mean, I understand, only sometimes it sure seems to me it's a curse to be a man."

"It's no easier being a woman," someone muttered, "and that's the choice."

"There's a third," Peter offered. "You could be neuter."

"God forbid."

"You're right." Peter rubbed his forehead but was careful not to brush away his tears.

I cannot with authority express the underlying nature of men's consciousness raising groups. My experiences with them are still too limited, and my approach to them, I suppose, still too diffident. The men with whom I spoke are well aware of America's pains and inequities, and where in contemporary history this renewed concern with masculinity and maleness fits. They are well aware too, of the hierarchies of human and social needs and where in these hierarchies a weekly or twice monthly men's group meeting might be placed. They are concerned with and troubled by the realities of contemporary socialization practices, and the definitions of maleness and femaleness that institutions offer and that people abide by. They understand the hurt of exclusion and oppression; they struggle with the ironies of their supposedly easy and superior status.

Especially interesting to me was the common concern of these men with exposing private anguish and confronting the sexist patterns of institutions, while at the same time minimizing the public attention that their groups received. Clearly, they understood how threatening their personal and collective discoveries may be to some people, especially those who uphold the ethic of acting cool, or those who continue to believe that men must mask feelings, honor sheer cognitive and analytic operations, and avoid subjective enterprises, unless of course they belong to that special breed known as artists.

The experiences with the men in these various groups were not couched in the rhetoric of guilt over the evils attributed to well-to-do, educated, articulate white men, although this topic appeared in one form or another everywhere. Conceptually, their concerns were with families, schools, institutions, groups, and the ways in which helping relationships—be they underwritten by the church, education, psychiatry, social work, counseling, not to mention work and marital relationships and simple friendships—might be enhanced by men's consciousness raising groups. In a more spiritual sense—and there is such a sense in most of these groups—the concern is with men and women, and the necessity of relationships being predicated on care and compassion. And if this sounds foolish, or poetic, or what in my day we used to call "simpy," if it sounds like a concern more appropriately associated with women, then the age-old stereotypes do in fact remain, and the need for men's groups and a men's movement is affirmed.

O
ne of the more well-known actions of the modern Civil
Rights movement has been the large-scale attack on
American educational programs and school systems.
Millions of dollars have sloshed around the United States as
city and township officials, along with governmental or university consultants, plan changes, adjustments, perhaps even
revolution of a sort. Sadly enough, the results of most of
these programs seem minimal, at times even retrogressive. To
become a success, a program for change, for the improvement
of educational environments for blacks and whites must be
nothing short of fantastic. It should occur, moreover, in a
large city where the national media can pick it up and make a
story of it. Stories of black-white confrontations, incidents,
school closings, police intervention, walk-outs, and personal
resignations are common; but a glow of change for the better
is rare in what are called "backlash prone" communities, even
though some blacks in fact meet with receptive administrators and teachers who are not victims of guilt and defensiveness. It is still more rare for these meetings to produce an
enduring program for significant change in the lives of those
who daily share a school's facilities and spirit.

Perhaps it says something about America that these stories
do not make news, and that the communities from which they
come receive little federal support and minimal university interest. Indeed, what we usually know about these communities is what our prejudices and stereotyping apparatus tell us.
But the stories and the communities are there, deserving recognition.

The sprawling "bedroom community" of Bristol Township,
Pennsylvania, containing Levittown's 17,000 homes, has a
population exceeding 67,000. Because of its location, many
Bristol Township husbands commute to Philadelphia to the
south and to Trenton to the north. Some even park their cars
at the Trenton railway station and ride to New York City five
days a week. Of the township's children, over 13,000 attend
one public school or another and therefore come under the
watchful eyes of the school superintendent and his or her associates in the Harry S. Truman Administration Building.
About seven percent of these students are black; but more
significantly, enough of the township's families reveal a level
of poverty sufficient to earn the district an entitlement under
ESEA Title 4 allocation.

Not to be confused with the town of Bristol, Bristol Township remains essentially a working-class community, although a middle class exists. "The residents of Levittown are working class too," someone said, "even though they'll tell you they're middle class." The township also has its areas of poverty. Its racial and ethnic struggles in and out of school are supported, even nourished, by its proximity to Philadelphia and Trenton, a fact which makes many people refer to this community as "backlash prone" and ripe for "productive" social change strategies. It is the kind of community where things can blow at any moment, and partly because of this and partly because of what's happening in America, Bristol Township sought assistance and admitted to its need for change. Remaining loyal to a belief that "the United States is still an 'open society' in which it is possible to rise in social class and achievement, provided that the tools needed to do so have been acquired as a result of education," school administrators made several major alterations.*

First, the township built more schools; to be precise, fifteen in the last seven years. This in addition to the two parochial high schools and two elementary schools built over the same period. It also improved a technical school finished in 1958, where thirty trades are taught under the combined efforts of six school districts. It established an opportunity class for pupils separated from their regular schools for disciplinary reasons, in an effort to return these students to their home classes. Furthermore, it launched a community school program in which parents and teachers together devised and conducted projects for the entire community. Activities like movies, roller skating, Black Studies League meetings, and sewing classes emerged in a school which stayed open to its people from 8 A.M. to 10 P.M., six days a week, twelve months a year. Considering the high tax rate of the community and its tremendous growth despite the lack of major industries, these are striking accomplishments.

Second, it rearranged the population in some of its schools when it became obvious that the overcrowding (almost forty percent) of black students in the Lafayette and Maple Shade schools was not only intolerable to many white teachers and parents, but a violation of the recommendations documented in the oft-quoted Coleman Report.† Reading, citing, and in-

*"Bristol Township School District Program," 1969, p. 26.
†James Coleman, et al. *Equality of Educational Opportunity.* Washington, D.C.: U.S. Government Printing Office, 1966.

corporating the research of Coleman, Robert Havinghurst,
Allison Davis, and Martin Deutsch, the various school administrators no longer could perpetuate institutions where the "disadvantaged" grew nowhere together. As they themselves wrote: "Society as we know it now postulates adult success upon the same traits required for school success. The successful adult, in terms of existing society, will be he who is relatively verbal, who relates well to others, who is clean and neat, possesses the whole range of middle-class mores and who, in addition, has achieved some mastery of the academic. . . . In general, the authorities agree that the greater the concentration of disadvantaged children, the less chance there is for the school to have a positive effect" (pp. 4, 5). So, under pressure from local residents and supported by distant intellectuals, they bused!

Before dispersing the disadvantaged, they considered building more schools or school additions, instituting more portable classrooms, split class sessions, and providing extra staffing. But economic constraints pointed to busing. It meant disrupting families and placing blacks in previously all-white schools. As a result of busing, the percentage of blacks in the overcrowded schools decreased by a little less than ten percent, although none of the receiving schools wound up with more than nine percent black or six percent so-called disadvantaged. Still, the move was costly, daring, and pleasantly, uncontested. Quite a change from the agonizing nights when bitter families swarmed around the first Levittown house to be occupied by a black family, threatening violence, while others stationed themselves on the home's front lawn, pledging to protect the brave people inside. Quite a change, too, from not so many years ago when some outraged teachers blew the whistle on school board members attempting to sell the principal's job, an action which led the district attorney to arrest five board members and convict two of them. It was a horrible scandal, replete with traps set with marked bribe money. It meant a drastic dip in the value of Bristol Township's stock, and equally important, in its morale.

Third, the school district formed an Intergroup Education Committee which sponsored speakers and worked on curriculum changes and summer Youth Study programs, and then turned to examine the tensions, the inevitable racial unrest and anger that had grown to impressive proportions. It's happening all over the country, so we shouldn't be surprised," one teacher had remarked. "We're no worse off than any-where else. We've got our good and our bad elements."

They were not omnipresent, these tensions, but some events in the preceding years bothered the people of the county, and something had to be done. There was talk, for example, of militant community organizing going on in the Terrace, one of the region's black communities, of night fights between police and students, and of an invasion of activists from Philadelphia and Trenton "stirring up unrest" in the three areas where black concentration was highest. Even black first, second, and third graders challenged their teachers by banding together on the playfields and insisting that everyone call them the "Black Butterflies." Then came the action.

The story at Franklin Delano Roosevelt Junior High School began on a day whose date few white administrators now re-member exactly. Blacks, however, recall the day as the anni-versary of Malcolm X's death. On that morning, thirteen students refused to attend their homerooms. As administra-tors recount it, the students claimed the day a holiday and insisted that their parents wanted them home. Phone calls re-vealed the opposite. Some mothers were confused, but in the main, all wanted their children at school. The students perse-vered; the principal gave them a choice and they left, their strength and support growing. Immediately, temporary sus-pensions were issued, but within a few days, the students had returned, and the social temperature of Bristol Township climbed.

The drama and tension in schools is always visible. Teach-ers can spot students "looking for trouble," and can feel the quivering petulance in the halls as students, five abreast, march to class bragging of their militancy, and at times, exhibiting a ferocious arrogance. Even the architecture of halls contrib-utes to the uneasiness, for as corridors come together in a "T," hundreds of people are thrown together. A scramble be-gins near the library or "lav," and blacks make pledges to sit together in classes where, at last, discipline becomes an al-most impossible norm.

Then, at last, the eruption, in the second week of May. A black girl "bucks the line" in the cafeteria. A white teacher tells her to go back and wham, the teacher hits her. Two oth-er girls rush to the student's defense. The three are suspended, one for the entire year. "To hear the black leaders, you'd think the teacher hit the girl with her chin," someone recalled.

In fact, the black community was more than a trifle aroused.
A group of "Hell's Black Cobras," young adults, eighteen to twenty-five, hung around the school grounds, "denim jackets and all . . . mouthy individuals they were. . . . " Eventually the police entered, and again black leaders intervened. The police were unhappy with their charge of keeping only "proper personnel" in the schools; the teachers seemed uneasy about the presence of any outsiders; the black community was upset over the perceived Uncle Tom-ness of their once-admired leaders who apparently were selling them out; and the black students exploded with demands for reinstatement of their sisters, more black teachers and counsellors, changes in the dress code, the works!

As bad as it was, it could have been worse. What helped was the sensitivity and understanding shown by administrators and teachers in their negotiations with students, parents, and community leaders. There was reportedly little of the usual rush to "call the cops," hunt the villainous school rebels, and bounce as many as one rightly could. Somehow punishment seemed far less important than communication, and somehow too, administrators and teachers seemed prepared. In fact they were prepared, but not as trained soldiers guarding the walls of a fortress.

Behind the preparation was their experience with Human Relations Training Laboratory groups and an offshoot, the Intergroup Education Committee. Bristol Township had discovered these groups and had been convinced of their efficacy. And many educators had grown to admire Dr. Max Birnbaum and his staff who, by the time of the incidents, had begun to lead several groups in two- and five-day sessions. To appreciate the impact of these groups on such situations of racial unrest requires brief mention of group work in the context of school systems. Generally, the scope of group techniques and purposes, philosophies and styles has become so variegated, that few people can say they truly understand just what they're "buying" when offered human relations groups.

In *Personal and Organizational Change through Group Methods*,* Professors Edgar H. Schein and Warren G. Bennis delineate four types of laboratory group procedures, each of which, not so incidentally, corresponds to variations in social and political approaches to change. The first emphasizes personal learning and includes techniques geared toward those well-

*New York: John Wiley, 1965.

known ideals of growth, personal emergence, or self-actualiza-tion. Based on work relationships, the second type stresses ex-aminations of interpersonal relations in a context of improving work efficiency among employees or colleagues. A third type is aimed at improving interpersonal communication generally, irrespective of one's work and social relationships "on the out-side." Intergroup relationships, such as those between blacks and whites, constitute the fourth type.

With any of these basic group definitions, group goals must also be articulated. Who or what is the ultimate client: the participant or in some indirect way, the social system in which he or she survives? What is the focus of learning? Should it be the individual participant, his or her relationship with tempo-rary group fellow members, or the association between groups in a community? Then, what should be the level of learning? Increased awareness, attitude change, an alteration in competence levels, or some admixture of all of these? As Schein and Bennis make plain, consideration of just this sort must be mapped out before group programs are undertaken and prospective staff are trained or prepped for a particular client, be it a business, factory, or school system. Without doubt, the status, competence, personality, and professional background of group leaders will greatly affect the outcome of any group. But without an underlying philosophy, groups have been known to be little more than "turn on's," happy, exciting experiences which in the long run have minimal ef-fect both on the person and the system in which he or she works, although participants might state that the experience, whatever it meant, was worth a million dollars.

For the most part rejecting the concepts and language of sensitivity or pure self-learning groups, Max Birnbaum and his staff arrived in Bristol Township insisting that group en-counters must include all members of the school community, particularly the people at the top, and must be oriented to the social system context and actual problems faced by indi-vidual school personnel in their respective schools. In short sessions, they argued, sudden and slick social interventions and references to psychodynamics only make participants more defensive and more resistant to learning. Furthermore, hate sessions, radical confrontations, soul searching, or what-ever they are called these days, cannot adequately help teachers comprehend the constraints on principals and superintendents or offer easy solutions to structural inadequacies in classrooms and governing boards.

If there is a technique to these groups, it rests on Birnbaum's and his assistants' capacity not only to hear the problems of participants, but to honestly reveal their own inabilities, ambivalences, even prejudices and elitist attitudes. Some would call it role modeling, but the styles of leadership displayed, generating as they do love one minute, hate the next, suspicion one day, doubt that night, involvement the next morning and adoration with questioning that afternoon, make the groups alive, vital, but not frightening to the point that persons slump by the wayside. It's easy to unzip people, harder to zip them up again, still harder to integrate their sentiments into the work and systems of work from which they cannot retreat and from which they derive definitions for their lives.

It is for this reason that a complete system approach was stressed involving all school personnel and all layers of society. As Birnbaum has written, "No organizational change will occur until all, or almost all of the persons who may resist change have been readied for innovation." A piecemeal or partial enterprise cannot take root. Importantly, Birnbaum's notion of training focuses on "personal growth for organizational adaptation to change and not on personal growth alone." Thus, it is neither pure problem-oriented nor therapeutic in purpose or in execution. Rather, what Bristol Township school personnel experienced were human relations training laboratory sessions simultaneoulsy focusing upon institutional and personal resistance and restraint to change. This means that participants had to understand the contexts in which their friends (and enemies) worked so that they could appreciate the pressures from within and from without the school system sustained by all of its members.

Unlike certain "sensitivity groups," the questions and problems explored became highly specific. Many models of group experiences where emphasis rests more on interpersonal sensitivity and personal growth could not be followed, as they could not deal with educational change in socially charged areas. The proverbial touching and feeling groups, or more orthodox T-groups in which issues of authority and intimacy are "explored" and "worked through," are not necessarily dysfunctional, but they do seem less suitable for the needs of most school systems requiring change. Similarly, it was Birnbaum's belief that "confrontation sessions" where truly angry or role-playing angry blacks intimidate whites also do not work, since the natural defensiveness makes participants even less willing to accept change and less able to see the confrontation in the context of daily school business and work relationships.

The overarching consultation strategy in Bristol was to work on major resistances to change in all school personnel. Where prejudices served and reinforced the status quo, they had to be gently exposed, legitimized in order to reduce defensiveness, fear of exposure and guilt, and then worked with in terms that would make change possible. The major goal of the laboratory sessions was to help administrators and teachers reduce their fears of and resistances to "appropriate" and "needed" changes in teacher-student and administrator-student relationships.

Today there is enormous confusion and misunderstanding about group work and variations in purpose and style. For participants in a potential group experience, this confusion ultimately leads to fear. To school superintendents, the publicity leads to distrust and doubt, two prominent obstacles to a project depending not only upon a superintendent's approval, but on his or her willingness to participate and to urge the entire staff to follow. Because of the publicity surrounding laboratory group experiences, it is not at all preposterous for a superintendent to believe that group work means lying on soft ground, touching and feeling, while black and white students cry out from the rooms and corridors of overcrowded schools. Perhaps these other kinds of sensitivity training would help, but they were not in fact what Birnbaum's staff proposed.

The plan for Bristol Township called for each of approximately 800 people (700 staff and 100 community representatives) to partake in one of two forms of groups. One form, for selected school leaders, teachers, and principals, would be five-day workshops stressing leadership skills and special sensitivities for handling minority group problems. According to the proposal, these people would return to their schools as trained cadres working "actively to create a climate of mutual respect and good will, [also making] themselves available to staff, students and school community when problems arise in the human relations areas." Cadres were to provide a model for teachers subsequently going through laboratory sessions. Furthermore, cadres were to play an important role in the Intergroup Education Committee. Chosen in part because they were neither severe in their racial attitudes nor excessively liberal, cadre members were to work implementing change procedures. Their job was a difficult one, for as one teacher suggested while laughing over the seeming impossibility of modeling himself after his teacher, "we were supposed to be miniatures of Birnbaum, 'mini-Maxes,' as it were."

The second type of group experience, two-day workshops, was intended for the remaining people, including selected parents, community leaders, and police. Ideally, even these quickie sessions would "heighten staff awareness of human relations problems," and increase their "facilities for dealing with tensions and incidents that arise from majority-minority relations."

Here, then, lay not only a plan for dealing with unrest, but also a representative example of the majority of American schools' reactions to unrest, and a circumscribed philosophy for treating it. The name of the game was to reduce racial incidents, avoid police intervention, keep schools open, and ameliorate as best as one could, situations where overly angry demands led to harsh disciplining. Some argued that such techniques as group encounters maintained the status quo and thus merely lessened the frequency of racial incidents. Others felt that perhaps these techniques were a first step toward real change. Still others could not see any connection between the techniques and radical community transformation, which ultimately would render violent protestations obsolete and human relations training laboratories anachronistic.

One does not know whether these types of political philosophies had even been considered by the thirty people who, for those two days, had been relieved of their duties so that they might "encounter one another" in the large dining room on the second floor of the Bristol Motor Inn. At about nine o'clock in the morning they came, a bit nervous, to commence whatever it was they were about to commence. Their group consisted of five nonpublic school people, eight district education specialists (like librarians and music teachers), one principal, and sixteen teachers. There would be teachers in this group for whom blacks and Jews, as well as the concept of welfare, were totally foreign "items" before their arrival in

Bristol not so many years ago. But as someone advised, "The community is filled with people who prefer to do the right thing." So, the administration was willing to pay the thirty dollars per day to each substitute filling in for teachers taking part in the group.

Up until now, few staff members had refused assignment to a group, and only one had seriously complained after completing a workshop. At worst, they were out of school for a couple of days, being paid, and not losing an evening or a weekend. Slowly then, they chose a chair from among the many placed around tables which had been arranged in a large rectangle, the center being open. In front of them, almost like at the United Nations, name placards were stationed, and at one end, in casual dress, sat their two leaders, Birnbaum and his assistant, James Small. Along one side of the room a waitress arranged coffee, tea, and sweet rolls on a narrow table. I sat along this same side, removed from the group but still in full view.

To describe in detail what transpired during these days is perhaps a violation of ethics and promises, a disclosure of materials presumably confidential. Without breaking a trust, some things, however, may be reported. In the main, Max and Jim, as they were instantly called, spent the entire first day, from nine in the morning until ten at night, interviewing all thirty people, one by one. Others, too, joined in with the interviewing, reacting, probing, asking, giggling. But it was the leaders who cajoled, pushed, provoked, commiserated, and revealed so much of themselves that others could not help but speak of the poverty they had tasted, their anger at being called a "wop" or "kraut," the tensions between people from hard and soft coal mining regions, their conflicts about blacks or young people generally, or the reluctance to identify their religion. They spoke in these interviews, of trying to be fair with all students, taking and treating them one by one as they came along, and their assuredness that prejudice is learned at home, rarely in the school.

Interviewing individuals within the group setting as all the others listen provides case material, as it were, for later discussion. The procedure has three major objectives. First, the interviews make it easier for persons to speak of ethnic and racial differences and attitudes without some of the tensions normally experienced in everyday social intercourse. Second, they enable participants to understand how influential their own religious and ethnic backgrounds have been in shaping their attitudes and actions, and how different these backgrounds are from others' backgrounds. Third, interviews elicit personal information which helps to generate mutual trust and cohesiveness among members.

For the most part, the technique of interviewing involves "role-modeling," a process in which leaders demonstrate and confess to their own insecurities, conflicts, and prejudices and thereby help participants to publicly admit to their own failings and uncertainties. Not until their collective admissions are gathered and examined will the participants be willing to study the consequences of their feelings and the "normal social actions" which follow them. During the interviewing, care is taken to assure participants that while the group effort is directed toward school and social problems, there remain large discrepancies between the anger of the aggressor and that of his or her victim. Ideally, interviewing brings out the singular identity of each participant, including the leaders, only to have these identities merge into a web of enduring trust and promise for change. Group interviewing requires a delicate skill in encouraging openness while avoiding characteristic psychotherapeutic interventions. In the end, the personalities, temperaments, perhaps even the charisma of leaders, may be the essential energy igniting and maintaining the force of such a procedure. But the energy is clearly wasted if, for even a moment, the context of school and the notion of change are lost or submerged.

Within minutes of commencing, the group had used the interview "data" to charge into discussions of sex, birth control, sterilization programs, and the earlier and earlier dates of the onset of menstruation. Everyone, presumably, seemed to know the statistics of six months earlier every ten years. It has almost become a symbol of precocity, the physiological analog of premature political sophistication and knowledge. It relates, too, to male and female aggression, sexual and otherwise. Then, through what some might call denials, came the inevitable tensions of black and white, rich and poor, old and young, male and female, teacher and student, parent and child, single and married, and always the leaders urging a testing of conflict, but never the opening of personal scars. Just enough, somehow, so that by the next day, one could ask about such matters as interracial dating or one's own experiences with prejudice. Just enough persuasive joking and nagging, advancing and receding, to make it possible to imagine perhaps, what it is to be the single black person in a classroom, the boy called "kike," or the girl never asked for a date. Just enough to permit people to tell why regulations and order mean so much, and why manners and sacred values often overshadow human expansiveness, creativity, and adventure. When a dead end seemed imminent, one of the leaders would recapitulate and underline the feelings toward black students expressed by some of the teachers. He would remind the group of an unspoken fear of black reprisal or the difficulties involved in bending over backward toward blacks, or not bending at all.

Noticeable relief spilled into the room when the leaders consented to a coffee break or lunch time, but somehow the group, the social system, the all-of-them-together, had been born. The hours since the morning meant history, the medium for recollection and trust. The hours in the future meant the moment when the interviewing radar would get to me. In the afternoon, television and newspapers were blamed for exacerbating racial tensions, which now, as an irrepressible melody, danced in and out of the group's rhetoric and psyche, returning unexpectedly in a discussion of athletics or the meaning of manhood. Or maybe it would come from out of the mist of an intentional silence layed softly by the leaders as a blanket on which to spread one's fears and hopes.

The group began to feel the age difference between its members. The younger ones perceived so much change in their students, the older ones saw the same thing in slightly varied form. The kids are tougher now, they'll hit you, their manners are bad, they seem ungrateful. But we don't seem as confident as our parents seemed.

"Our parents changed and we're going through exactly what they went through. They used to hit kids, you know. Today, kids threaten us and we can't retaliate. The parents and students don't have enough respect for us. Even the parents attack authority." Then there was silence and it was Coke time. The afternoon was moving on, and while a few members talked among themselves somehow keeping out the group "noises," others appeared more energized by the drama. Still others had tuned out altogether.

Just before dinner, tides of denial returned. People spoke of their home towns where prejudices rarely existed; at least they did not know of them. They spoke as well of the town's

Jew Hill or its Italian ghetto. Then the undercurrent of black-
ness-whiteness returned. It was back now in terms of social
mobility, ethnic groupings, patronage systems, rural-urban
comparisons, and status inconsistencies. Max and Jim spent
some time lecturing on sociology and the multiplicity of values in a pluralistic society. They reminded the group of students' rights and duties, and promptly the discussion turned
to Bristol Township for the first time. Race and economic
distinctions singed the fabrics they described; animosities
were unleashed toward the Jewish country club set and the
self-styled middle-class smugness of working-class Levittown.
At the nineteenth person interviewed, first mention was
made of their own families. They spoke of their children,
then of themselves as parents and teachers. Some were struck
anew by the "science of teaching." They reeled from someone's insistence that we have not yet learned how to teach. If
we knew what we were doing, someone said, we could help
low-motivation students. They all agreed. There are no adequate measurements for discriminating between students, but
there isn't enough money either. In Pennsylvania, a man reported, a family of four requires $9,100 a year, but what
teachers make that much? It's amazing. Through busing,
blacks have achieved greater mobility than we have.

Outside, where the even traffic flow moaned on, the sky
darkened. Everyone was exhausted, eager for a respite, a
drink, a meal. Everyone felt urges to return, urges never to return. At dinner, the leaders reiterated the notion of system
level run groups, and the necessity of keeping group process
and content together. The problems confronted by teachers
must be dealt with directly, but no one must be pushed, especially not by liberal warriors. Growth must be enhanced in
a way that does not interfere with one's job. When change is
required, those yielding power must be implicated, and the
system, not the individual, treated.

Just before the evening session, Max and Jim reiterated
group strategies: they would stay with materials of the here
and now and seek focal figures who not only would express
the feelings and attitudes of others, but who, when they
moved, would budge others. Expectations were not to be
raised too high, or the workshop's effects would not take hold.

During the evening session, younger members recounted
their teaching problems. Challenged by students who had
been socialized to merely absorb, like sponges, the teachers

were hard put to explain why grammarial laws insist that "I ain't got none" is eternally incorrect. Grammar, said one, should only be taught when thoughts become entangled or constricted and thinkers distracted. People stirred as two young teachers spoke of the intimate trust they sought in relationships with students. Dress codes were discussed along with sex education anecdotes, and then, while the men and women in the Bristol Motor Inn Bar below sipped drinks, upstairs in the group, discussion of racial tensions returned. The group was just beginning to label differences and "get these differences out on the table." The leaders moved with special prudence, abiding by their own laws of where one can push and where one cannot. They hunted focal persons, all the while watching for others who listened more to one member than to another. Aware of their own resistances, the group moved slowly. People were tired, enervated, anxious to leave. They had momentarily forgotten that tomorrow meant resuming. The room emptied quickly; they were almost running away from Max and Jim.

Fresh the next morning, the group commenced its second and final day. "Old friends" now convened, some seeking new seating arrangements almost as if their identities might be strengthened in a different location. The dress was less formal; some of the men arrived in open sport shirts. The group was quickly at work, the discussions more open, more penetrating, the anger and defiance direct and exposed, the resistances shriveling a bit around the edges. Soon Max and Jim divided the group in two, Max herding high school teachers and principals into another upstairs dining room, Jim remaining with the elementary school personnel.

The smaller groups focused on immediate problems; certain students were mentioned by name. A story was told of a young black man who had been popular and well accepted, but who, after graduation, opposed the school because he saw the stains of racism. Max tried to portray how a young black person's sense of alienation and discrimination cannot be dissolved by football heroics or dancing skills, even when these skills mean fame among white girls. Others joined in, confessing prior misunderstandings, fears, and antipathies, but themes of guilt were avoided. Max recounted the story of Freud who wrote that if he had had his choice, he would have analyzed teachers because they are parents without being parents, and because their jobs cut across all of society.

For a moment there was silence; then they were back at
work. They were back at a brand of work they had not known, possibly with an energy and drive that seemed to them uncanny, magical. The tough were becoming tender; the tender admitting hardness and bitterness. The leaders spoke more of themselves, their early experiences, their hostilities and sadness. They assured their groups that losing control in a classroom does not mean losing authority, or face, for that matter. Mutterings were heard about being the classroom's dominant figure, the most respected, the one who lays down law and makes others obey.

Soon it was afternoon. The subgroups reassembled. People seemed to be sensing the end; the edges began to fit together. A discussion about prayer in the public schools exploded, but several group members quieted the issue. Everyone was jabbering about individual differences: Jewish bibles, King James bibles, Black bibles, Mohammed bibles, no bibles. Several men threw morality at the leaders who threw back reprints of an article on pluralism. The group had caught on. It took many hours and four different coffee breaks, but they were appreciating human differences and needs and the fact that while some people will kill to eliminate these differences, others might kill just to preserve them. They were listening, laughing, making sure they would not forget certain special phrases.

Woman: The problem of the world is that they're tearing down things we found security in.
Max: What about Catholics? They're really going through problems.
Man: We're just shaking out the weak ones, Max.

Then, it was over. Some were glad to leave. Some presumably found it useful, others not. "I'm going to look a little harder." "I'm neutral." "I'm going to have to cooperate more. It's going to be hard." "I don't know what I'll get from it 'til later." "Does everything have to collapse before new things can come?" "It's going to take some real hammering out; some real gutsy dialogue." "Compare us with your other groups." "That's like a girl saying do you love me more than anyone else?" "We'll absorb change. Our country will be able to absorb all of this. You just wait and see."

Then they were gone. Max and Jim had shaken hands and departed, their car streaking down the Pike to a weekend group workshop in western Pennsylvania. Each of us trudged out, our thoughts centered on how to continue and on figuring out just what had happened in those upstairs rooms. Many of us would have given anything to know whether the future might be altered by these two days.

In later talks with teachers I learned that these thoughts do not diminish even months after the group experience. For the cadres, the impact remains uncertain and their feelings of inadequacy remain prominent. "But still we've got to do something; something is better than nothing. At least things have been put out on the table and we can speak openly of black and white issues." While for some the groups stimulate racial feelings, the effect of social class and ethnic differentiations also becomes significant. But their concerns lie with race and the miniscule happenings which can, in a flicker, turn to war.

Reactions to the groups or perceptions of others' reactions are yet to be studied systematically. On the basis of a few conversations, it seems that some find the experience too blunt, wasteful, and irrelevant. Others find it valuable, useful, though anxiety provoking, helpful, morale building, morale breaking, too antidisciplinary, too much in favor of the kids.

For one teacher, what is needed more than anything else "is the courage to love people and to touch them. This is really the Judeo-Christian ethic. People make assumptions and act as though the assumptions are reality. Demonstrations are based on the assumption that 'they' won't listen. . . . The people above you and below you must be treated with love." For another teacher, no group could possibly counteract the pitiful salaries, low prestige, and inadequate training of teachers. Schools, moreover, suffer from the lack of "intellectual" as well as personnel facilities, like five guidance counselors in a school of over 2,000 pupils. Adminstrators who overplay dress code regulations and force teachers to adhere to their curriculum were not moved by the groups as much as those predisposed to change.

Many teachers, however, disagreed with these sentiments, arguing that the groups were instrumental in helping some schools over a hump of racial unrest: "I don't know what the groups meant. I do know I cried when a black teacher told of listening to his black students who made him feel glad he was black." "Say, you know who got a lot out of the group, is Joe Ruane. You ought to speak with him. He's been continuing with group things."

Joseph John Ruane, the principal of F.D.R. Junior High School, has indeed been continuing just fine. The story of the change in "Karate Joe," as he once was called, borders on the apocryphal, and no one treasures this more than Joe. It was in his office that the suspension of the three girls took place. It was in his schoolyard that police stalked about keeping the Cobras away from an already "too tense situation."

Years ago, Joe Ruane was a tough man, a man who would just as soon shove a kid up against a locker and savor the crash, than speak with him. There were no discussions, no negotiations with "Karate Joe" in those days. The door to his office stayed tightly shut, opening only for disciplinary problems. Then a teacher would come in, complain or cry, and Joe would storm out to settle the matter. But no more. Discipline problems, naturally, persist, but Joe Ruane has changed. His door stays open, and when he cannot negotiate with tolerance, he is likely to turn to an assistant principal "who'll inevitably be seen by the kids as Mr. Nasty."

More often, however, Joe will turn over discipline problems to his Intergroup Advisory Council, a group of twenty-two thoughtful ninth graders. Several times each year, this group of black and white students has to make serious decisions regarding school disruptions. One year the issues were fighting in the halls and skirmishes after basketball games. In both cases, the council, given full control by Ruane and teacher Arnold Hillman who sits as faculty representative, devised disciplinary procedures which worked. Voting themselves Traffic Control Monitors, they hammered out anticipated tensions that would emerge when whites went to repress blacks and vice versa. As for the gym episode, they set rather extensive attendance limitations which, not ironically, affected several of their own members.

To generate the council, several student leaders, aided by Ruane, Hillman, and science teacher Albert Ulbinsky—all graduates of the five-day leadership workshop—planned a general student election, replete with area redistricting in order to achieve greater black representation. In the end, fifteen whites and eight blacks were elected. The actions of the council, their deliberations over drug abuse, racial unrest, smoking, quality of teaching, and physical discipline reverberated throughout the community. It is a respected group, eager to tackle any problem from the Cobras to filth in the cafeteria. Devotedly, Hillman meets regularly with the council, his "points of personal privilege" often underscoring its work, but never undermining it.

A noticeable pride hovers around Joe Ruane's office. "No one used to be more bullheaded than I," Joe has announced. "The muscle worked. Now I see it's bad. I can deck 'em, but it isn't going to prove anything other than the fact that the kids are right about the establishment." It is precisely this demeanor that makes that pride so real. Apparently others have felt it too; recent flare-ups at the neighboring Delhaus School prompted a request for Ruane to speak with parents. Quite a tribute from one principal to another.

Ruane knows teachers want specific solutions to their problems. He knows too that he must encourage parents and teachers to speak up against the school even if this means minor confrontations and uncomfortable realignments. He realizes that he must jeopardize himself at times, and so he has. He wants his personnel to speak of their feelings about race because he has learned that lurking animosities can result in police invasions. He is willing to confront his own prejudices; and even more, he is proud that temporary suspensions have significantly decreased and that there are youngsters in his school who trust him and would dare reveal to him their hurts and tears.

As dramatic as the story of Joe Ruane is, two major community events provide even better evidence of the social efficacy of the Human Relations Training groups. The first had to do with black youths arrested for stealing during a football game between archrival schools, Woodrow Wilson and Bishop Egan. Presumably some students had snatched purses and had been seen "walking mysteriously" through the parking lot. Police arrived, and after the inevitable scuffling and screaming, seven persons were arrested. Five of these, juveniles, were released into the custody of their parents. The other two were charged with disorderly conduct, and one other was charged with resisting arrest and threatening a police officer. Bail for him, originally set at $2,000, was reduced substantially after black community leaders intervened.

Exacerbating this episode were the photographs accompanying the story in the *Bucks County Currier Times*. In the *A* edition, a rather ambiguous photograph showed a policeman either slugging a black youth in the stomach or grabbing and twisting his belt. Printing the same story, the *B* edition pictured one of the two injured policeman, a large gash on his

head. While the editor of the paper saw nothing unusual in
these photographs, several school representatives claimed they were inflammatory on the grounds that the *A* edition is purchased primarily in the black communities, the *B* edition in the working-class white communities.

The second community event involved two black students and a police cruiser. Heated words among them tripped off school tensions and for a while, it was more than a bit touchy in Bristol Township. Both of these events, however, were handled gently and passionately by teachers and administrators alike who, having been prepared somewhat by the Human Relations groups, demonstrated this preparedness by "hanging loose" and letting the students handle their own problems within the schools. In one case, students actually ran closed meetings, inviting school and community officials as they saw fit. In a second case, a police officer participating in a two-day school-community institute admitted that he could have exercised better judgment by responding less severely to the verbal provocations of angry young men. Student reaction to the football incident seemed especially significant, for while the situation remained touch and go, it never erupted. More importantly for school personnel, a sufficient number of students maintained a trust in administrators in the face of militant action by some community leaders.

Despite these promising results, the Bristol Township experiment could hardly yet be deemed "totally successful." No one can escape the ubiquitous bad press that poorer communities sustain almost every week. "Where money and influence exist," the superintendent said, "bad things don't make the papers." As for the groups, they can do just so much. The cadres are constrained by the new leaders' lack of experience in human relations work and teachers' natural resentment toward being "guided" by their colleagues.

But the greatest group experience, one administrator noted, cannot replace fine team teaching and curricula relevant for youth in a time of change, or simply "for kids with the intelligence God gave them. Social studies teachers should teach every controversial issue, but if the kids aren't mature, things can be a waste. You give *Hamlet* to everyone just because the curriculum calls for it, but it may not be relevant to all people."

Bristol's superintendent did not fear dress styles, music fads, beads, granny glasses, underground newspapers, long hair, or even Students for a Democratic Society. He had tenth-grade teachers reading theories of communism with their pupils, and independent study programs where heaven only knows what was being learned. He was proud of the thirty-five percent of Woodrow Wilson High School's graduating seniors who go on to some form of college, and the fact that Bristol Township is willing and able to hire good teachers, black and white. The content of his apprehension was predictable: "Things are bad, let's face it. If cities go down, we go down and the whole country goes down. Our major cities have to survive and we're not doing anything about it. College professors want to leave their summers free, so they run institutes just when high schools are letting out. So, we're on our own."

More generally, results of programs like the one in Bristol Township are always tentative, always in a delicate balance. As they say, "things could blow next week." So far, the approach taken has worked. Racial tensions have not erupted even in areas where hostilities and anger lurk almost everywhere. No one can yet claim that the groups significantly reduce individual prejudice, but groups do get the problems "on the table" and admitted to, and hopefully, this means that prejudiced attitudes and hostilities of this sort will not always control all behavior and all decisions. Social change, or more accurately system change, can occur, and it just may be occuring in Bristol Township. Nonetheless, one must ask whether political and social institutions will reinforce these changes or work to maintain that status quo which the groups hope to challenge.

"Tell me one thing," I was asked once by a young man in a ghetto area of Boston. "Do you ever come back? I mean, when you've finished with whatever you do, will you come back?" There is perhaps, a certain feeling of abandonment lurking in this sentiment. Each of us, in the manner that lives are led, does our work and moves on. As I watch a worker immersed in his trade, I often wonder if he has become so attached to one job that he finds it difficult to leave it upon completion. Does a psychiatrist dread the last visit of a patient? Who returns to check up on a job, or to inquire about the welfare of someone once called a client, or an acquaintance, the someone who provided the material for a research project or article?

It has been more than two years since I visited Bristol Township, Pennsylvania. While many of the recollections remain intact, I find I am barely able to place the year, or even the time of year of that trip. I had not the barest idea of what evolved in that community. I thought about the people there occasionally, and about the efficacy of the program, and, of course, about Max Birnbaum. Yesterday I called Bristol and asked to speak with the old superintendent of schools. "He no longer works here," came the response. "Would you like to speak with the present superintendent, Mr. . . .?" The principal of Woodrow Wilson High School had left the area too, but most of the others remained. Many had new positions. Many who had pledged to leave or to move up, still occupied their former jobs. Merely inquiring about these people made me feel a bit strange. Had I not, after all, written my story and moved on?

Programs of community social change, amelioration, whatever one calls them, are rarely undertaken by outsiders. It is the people who stay who sustain them. Often, the gist of a program, its execution or ideology dies not from a lack of interest or effort, but because what has been imposed cannot possibly be furthered by the people for whom it was initially prescribed. Elitism, self-aggrandizement, ignorance of areas, of people, of history, often combine to produce stunning plans, which, when actualized, fit a community of human beings about as poorly as a disheveled slum house fits the needs and dignity of a civilized person.

In Bristol Township, the Human Relations Training seems to have taken, almost as a skin graft might cover a gaping tear. Max Birnbaum's own work was concluded shortly after the time of my own visit. Since then the program has been expanded. The original cadre and its new trainees now run the groups, and all new teachers in the district are obliged to undergo a two-day sensitivity session prior to the commencement of the school year. In-service training also has been expanded. The Intergroup Council for parents and young people continues.

Where the program has evidenced its most significant expansion, however, is in the realm of training for "biculturalism in the classroom." The problem, as one old friend remarked, came down to, "What do I do in this bicultural classroom in which I now am as sensitive as hell?" To aid teachers, a Princeton professor was engaged by the school district to work on anthropological issues of biculturalism. A white professor from Trenton State was brought in to teach black history to teachers. Where Max Birnbaum brought humanity into the schools, the focus now had turned to content. David Riesman too, spent time in the region working with teachers on the problem of classroom content and curriculum.

So the work that began several years ago, the work of human beings that I witnessed in this small portion of eastern America, is very much alive today, although the tension between the races can hardly be dissipated by any T-group or training courses in black history. As much as we might wish, social structures, national politics, and a form of racism that pervades our culture are not about to give way to earnest sentiment or even dedicated local community work. Not yet, anyway.

A while ago there was a riot at Woodrow Wilson High School. Seven people were hospitalized due to what was called, "You know, the general racial business." No one, naturally, can re-create the history, the enormous number of events which come together to rip apart a school and those who gather there five days a week. Some of the factors had to do with demands made by militants, as they are always called, who gained control of the local NAACP office. The principal told the group that many of the demands were not in his purview. He had nothing to do, for example, with the hiring of teachers, black or white. On a Wednesday morning, ten black students had entered his office to recite their demands. The principal arranged for a meeting with school board members and district officials to be held on Friday. At that time, with everyone properly introduced, one student rose and read a statement indicating that talk was useless and that the blacks were leaving. On Monday morning, police arrested forty-five black students, including the original ten. The NAACP officers demanded that the school board respond publicly to a host of demands. Accepting the challenge, the board announced that there were more black teachers in the district than in the entire county. As for black literature, the board happily reported that the state's Human Relations Commission had visited Bristol Township seeking suggestions for a bibliography in light of its fine collection.

During this time, the Ku Klux Klan was active too. They founded a junior group, soliciting membership from among high school students, and drove around in black communities shooting children with beebee guns.

Still, there are some who feel it could have been worse.
Clearly, certain administrators did not perform as well as they might have, given the sensitivity training and the hundreds of hours spent considering how to handle such occurrences and how to help people to "get in touch with their anger." In a few schools, however, top administrators either ignored the human relations training or opposed it outright. Thus, some reactions were predictable.

James Small, who assisted Max Birnbaum during my stay in Bristol, was glad to hear from me. We had been out of touch for a long while. He knew only slightly about the township. No one from the Laboratory had visited Bristol since his part of the program had concluded. Jim knew of some of the local departures and through friends who had attended a summer training laboratory in Massachusetts, he had heard a bit about Bristol's development. He had been told that the program essentially was well established, although the schools in which principals had been "converted" were definitely faring better.

A follow-up study in fact had been undertaken. Birnbaum and Small had requested that a team from Boston University visit Bristol and conduct a thorough evaluation. The final report was mammoth but it disappointed quite a few people both in New York and in Bristol. A bit of attitude change data was included, but for the most part the report seemed overloaded with impressions. In the end, there was too little to go on. Taking some notes as the silences on the phone grew in length, I heard Jim Small say, "Thinking about Bristol is like thinking about history." It *was* like history. Like the history I could barely recall studying in junior high school; Venezuelan history or Peruvian history where perhaps a single name or date comes back for no good reason, and one spends his or her energies attempting to calculate in which year one studied these countries rather than groping for the events that describe that country's history.

Something always seems surrealistic about many programs for social change. The problems don't mesh, somehow, with their diagnoses or with the strategies used to implement change and ultimately bring progress. I recall hearing of a group of urban design researchers who received a grant of over one hundred thousand dollars. It was purely a planning grant, an amount of money allowing them to design ways to improve the housing conditions of the poor. Months later,

they proposed the idea of moveable walls, a tricky construc-
tion procedure that would permit people to rearrange their
internal environments and from this, gain, well, I'm not sure
exactly what. In response to the proposal I said that my own
home, with which I was utterly happy, had thick walls which
reeked of strength and permanence, and that I would need
dynamite to budge them. A young student sitting next to me
said, "Maybe we should start giving the poor their own grants
of one hundred thousand dollars." Someone next to him then
muttered, "If not that, at least give them the dynamite."

The issues are never perfectly summarized, even by notions
of full autonomy and the control of one's destiny. "We are
monitoring ourselves," an old Bristol friend told me. Then,
reflecting on Max, he added, "At some point, everybody has
to walk without the crutch." And so we all do. It is not sur-
prising, indeed it is expected, that Max and his colleagues, in
all this time, would be immersed in projects in Miami and
New York, and see Bristol as part of their history, a part of
their valued history. I, too, have gone on to new projects and
have crossed paths with people in other cities and towns. Importantly, however, the struggle in Bristol Township, without
romanticizing it, is a struggle perpetuated in part by precisely
this natural passage of human beings from one stage or one
client or one moment to the next. Few of us are able to sustain interest in one thing long enough to allow us to adhere
to a continuing life work.

Yet there remains a group of people in this country who
simply have no choice in the matter, and must sustain whatever their passage through life calls for. For some of them,
sensitivity training is a preposterous solution to their daily
despair. For some of them, the chance even to make a demand
seems to be an event that only God might have arranged. For
some, the arrival of Max Birnbaum in a forgotten township
meant that all at once living a life with dignity was possible.
Max understood how rage, confusion, and bitterness got in
the way of teaching. He never punished the teachers, but rather let them experience life as adults. Even if his stay in the
township was brief, he would at least achieve, for some, a
special feeling, a feeling of humanity, a feeling of self-discov-
ery, a feeling for the pain of another person.

The fact remains, however, that no one, despite an abun-
dance of personal sensitivity and renewed awareness, can ever

hold his or her head high until the weight of an entire society
is taken off his or her back. Until that time there will be people who will necessarily make demands and stalk out of meeting rooms leaving only the echo of their words, and with it, the import of their dreams.

One man took a fast look around and called it the world's largest bar mitzvah, ever. "The president went to his catering staff," he dreamed aloud, scanning the Olympia Bar for newcomers—the famous, the attractive, the minorities, whomever—"and said, 'Max, get 'em a hotel, two hotels, three, five hotels, anything they want. Let 'em eat and drink. Forget the money, Max. Show 'em movies, entertain 'em. But Max, no trouble. I don't want any trouble.' " The rest of us roared. Blacks roared, whites roared, the old roared, the young roared. A giant bar mitzvah with the confirmed being every child in America regardless of race, color. . . . Surely the metaphor was better or more optimistic than the description of the affair as a typical day in public school, a junior high student government meeting, a P.T.A. gathering that had metastasized, a Great White Film Festival, or a dress rehearsal for a national party convention.

The White House Conference on Children, 1970. Where can someone possibly begin to describe this unbelievable organism, this fantasy, this immersion into a contrived, hopeless, and yet tough and ultimately magnificent reality that 4,500 of us or so knew for one December week? To have been there was not only to have worked endless hours on forum reports and on the wording for legislation, nor for that matter to engage in the politics that overnight grew into a sometimes poignant, sometimes frail voicing of demands and despair. To have been there was to experience a cacophonous scenario; it was to witness lines upon lines of people making applications for something, waiting for a document or hot dog, wandering about looking for the Delaware, Alexandria, or Wilmington Ballroom. It was to fall over ten black boys in karate outfits, or a group of youngsters from Urbana carrying little violins, or watching everyone's costume change from Monday to Tuesday, the slick traveling suits becoming turtle necks and hippie slacks or dashikis, and the dresses giving way to pants ensembles or jeans.

To have been there meant being bombarded by a traffic jam of bodies and noises and smells, the booze flowing earlier and earlier each day, and the tobacco, more and more pungent. It was to be accosted by the academic, organizational, social work, or industrial pitchpersons in the lobbies, in the upstairs suites and exhibition halls flinging their appeals, notions, philosophies, books, games, machines, and toys—objects of brilliant color and extraordinary ingenuity. To walk

in and out of the conference rooms was to have a million
Christmasses blow up in your face. It all felt as though a pi-
ñata had finally broken and a technology of toys and educational materials—what are called visual aids—were raining
down from a bountiful heaven possessed by not-so-angelic
business people, intellectuals, and bureaucrats. Then there
were the rows upon rows of gadgets, kids working at type-
writers, phonographs, minicomputers, kids lying on the floor
on special childrens' mattresses under hot lights, dressed in
their convention finest, painting nontoxic images with nontoxic paint on special-strength paper. Little girls with bright
blue leotards and barely tried muscles, jumped on contrap-
tions that counted for them or spelled something, while older girls in black leotards revealing experienced, dependable
muscles led a southern Illinois dance troop out of a lavatory
toward the large stage where they would rehearse their performance for a minispectacular, "The Sounds of Children,"
two nights hence. Then, still other women, with sombreros
out to here and skirts up to there offered free cokes. "The
only free thing we got all week," someone would say angrily
two days later at a press conference.

America, or well, a certain sample of it anyway, had come
to Washington, most of them paying their own way (one hundred uninvited children arrived and lived in a nearby church),
to do business, to make politics, to care for children, and to
perpetuate or stabilize their own worlds back home in the
community, as we seem to be calling it more and more. They
had come to know the gleam of Washington spotlights and
even more, to get in on the action. There was almost an unspoken promise in those first Sunday and Monday hours that
the guts of America's social and economic politics might open
themselves to a rather nifty group of people. Just for a moment, it seemed that for once we might be on the inside looking out. After all, this was Washington and someone had
already reported that he was sure he had seen Jack Javits
milling among the crowd, or was it Birch Bayh? Or maybe it
was Daniel Schorr or Ron Nessen. "Yeah, Daniel Schorr. I
knew I knew that face." Were we then to be let in to the very
boiler room of the military industrial complex? Didn't Agnew
himself live in this hotel, or was that story about someone
getting off the elevator at the wrong floor and bumping into
this enormous 1930 Cagney movie bodyguard a fantasy? But
someone had sworn he'd seen Mr. Rogers and Captain Kanga-

roo walking right through the lobby of the Sheraton Park Hotel.

Some arrived Monday and therefore missed Sunday night's address by the president (now available on a little plastic record), which was simpy, brilliant, stupid, fabulous, surprisingly good, predictably bad. Others had been there since Saturday and even earlier, working with conference staff members on one thing or another. But this meant that the whole thing was rigged, arranged before one's arrival, structured by an elite group of real insiders, know-it-alls, presidential henchmen. Thus, everything, but everything was becoming political and politicized, for it was Washington, and no matter how one enters this city he or she has to pass some building or monument, some style of architecture or patch of urbanism that bespeaks bigness, power, and government. Furthermore, an often overly privileged media corps were present at the revolving doors to greet the delegates, and before anyone could even utter the words child or kid or day care, a message got out that the White House Conference on Youth, for the first time separated from the Conference on Children, would be held in Estes Park, Colorado on the top of a mountain so high and so far from anywhere that no one would need fear even the slightest repercussion. All the action there would merely die in a ruffle of echoes. ("When the concern for kids dies," someone said, "the society dies.")

The politics and style of it all, the imagined as well as real ambience of Washington, the look of the hotels and the frantic bell captains, conference staff, and the press dashing to cover a something that might be news, looking for a celebrity, a famous psychologist, Andrew Young, Morry Turner, Piri Thomas, the head of C.B.S.—wasn't that Marge Champion speaking with those theatrical types? —this was the door prize, the initiation, the introduction to a collection of people and groups, all of whom might have believed that a single, definable purpose or meaning might be found that would sanctify the titles or cities or organizations that shone in large, children's-size type on their badges, and that might actually make the days and the discussions cohere. But there would have to be a final act, one consummate bit of legislation, entertainment, drama, a slogan or gimmick that would tie everything together; something that would give the journalists their lead-in, something that would give everyone a tangible fistful of Washington action that they might take home to their families and neighbors, and who knows, perhaps to America's children as well. One final act fabricated by *them*, not by the president, not by the bar mitzvah caterers, the minipoliticians, or the public school hall guards and school committees. It would have to come. ("If we don't care for kids now," the man said, "they're going to kill us and we deserve to die.")

White House conferences on children and youth were established in 1909. James E. West, we learned, a Washington lawyer orphaned at age six, had planted the seed by suggesting to President Theodore Roosevelt that the government should ameliorate the conditions of America's orphans and destitute children. Some two hundred people attended that first meeting at the New Williard Hotel. Significantly there were women present, a few blacks, and some celebrities, notably writers. For whatever the reasons, it was decided that one conference every ten years would suffice and 1970, with all else that it meant, marked ten years since the previous White House Conference on Children and Youth, a conference which had prepared the Head Start program, now but a few years after its inception, in a precarious financial position.

Not too much fuss has been raised about this infrequent collective gesture toward children. Apparently those allowed to attend and the others who still might believe, as I did, that the conference takes place in the White House itself and thereby renders participants big shots for a week, have agreed that one week a decade is enough time to devote to our country's "wall-to-wall children," as a Kentucky conferee described them. Or, maybe it takes ten years to put into law what a conference decides should be put into law. Or, maybe the very word children implies that each generation may scrutinize its successors but once a lifetime. Then again, perhaps it takes a full ten years for the brain, blood, and heart cells to rejuvenate themselves and make it possible for one human being to attend his or her second White House Conference and be assured of sustained good health.

There are some—what are they called these days? Bleeding hearts, I think—who contend that the president is not overly sympathetic to children and other living things. Most assuredly, a president in the 1970s is no less complicated about offspring and future generations than the rest of us, even though particular life styles and characterizations suggest to us, the observers and self-appointed analysts, more or less compassion, more or less humanity. For a time it looked like 1970 might pass without the conference. But then, without fanfare, Stephen Hess, someone close to the president and a man of extraordinary energy and political competence, was asked to coordinate the conference. "I have asked Mr. Hess to listen well to the voices of young America," the president announced on December 5, 1969, "in the universities, on the farms, the assembly lines, the street corners."

That Hess was the man chosen by the president, that he was even known to the president, meant for some that he possessed and disseminated evil and that his purpose was to manipulate the convention in ways that would make it impossible for any serious work to be accomplished and any legislation to reach the floor of Congress. So, as is always the case when hordes of generous and still self-interested persons who pack anger, defiance, and long histories of tragedy in their suitcases along with their few changes of clothes come together, a single person is at once selected to be the culprit, the Man, the puppet, the devil. In this case Stephen Hess, not his staff, not his president, was unanimously appointed as the personification, the incarnation of evil, and just as foolishly, an apotheosis of children bubbled in the decadent halls of the freshly renovated Washington Hotel. ("You can't kid a kid," a woman said. "I'm with 'em. We got a great world coming up.") Within hours of one's arrival the rhetoric, expressions, and emotionality, the humor and vituperation were somehow contorted as though a mammoth family had been tugged out of place, causing parents everywhere to be deemed illegitimate and their children to be disenfranchised and called by the single word, orphan.

With about a year to prepare, although various states engaged in numerous preconference sessions, Mr. Hess pulled together a staff of people who could run a conference of grandiose proportions and "connect" with those people who "know children, who work with them, study, film, record, transcribe them, care, feel and politic for them, and often sadly enough, feel themselves to be child 'experts.'" His goals were to produce high-quality forum reports, demonstrate to the nation what the possibilities were for governmental level reform, and bring children's concerns to the front pages of newspapers where our present hot and sexy political action monopolizes public attention. Many of his chairpersons would lament that conference politics would keep the contents of forum reports out of the papers and the media people themselves out of the discussions. Mr. Hess himself would worry about a conference "biased in favor of innovation" and the friction caused by a lack of "mutuality of interests."

Nonetheless, in preparation, hundreds, probably thousands of individual credentials were sifted through, as well as the names of such institutions and agencies as U.C.L.A., Harvard, the Boy Scouts, the Red Cross, Planned Parenthood, National Urban League, YWCA, and the Jews and Catholics and Appalachians and New Yorkers, the browns, blacks, whites, the poor, well, not really the poor, but you know ("We do for foreigners what we don't do for persons at the conference"), and the rich and famous and powerful and powerless, and all the states and regions and planes of visibility, and Yale and Michigan and the American Diabetes Association and day-care people and the American Academy of Pediatrics, T-group people and T-grouped people, singers, dancers, and shrinks, everyone was there, selected by some incredible sorting procedure for this carnival, for this bar mitzvah, for this decennial work.

"Next week on our stage, a really big show." It was a young black man from Kansas standing in the lobby of the Hilton. "A really big, big show. Right here on our stage, the entire cast of the White House Conference on Children will be here along with Charlton Heston, Topo Gigo, and the stars of the Japanese road company of *My Fair Lady*. So drive carefully and goodnight." He raised a clenched right fist and grunted.

Clearly there were names that should have or might have been there that week. Perhaps they were asked and declined, or maybe they were proposed and rejected by a White House representative or group that presumably approved the names of certain prominent participants. It is difficult to know because stories don't always jibe and one must accept the knowledge that certain truths never get reported. All the same, while published documents reported at least three different numbers, twenty-six forum topics were selected as the organizing feature of the convention. Selected by the staff, the topics of each forum were meant to consider the lives of all children, the poor as well as the rich, those in rural areas as well as in cities. Each forum, furthermore, was grouped with associated forums to produce topic clusters. In all, six major clusters were formed with forum 26, Child Service Institutions: Meeting the Needs of the '70s, serving as its own cluster.

An Individuality cluster was comprised of forums titled, "I'm Me," "Emergence of Identity: The First Years," "Expressions of Identity: The School-Aged Child," and "Crisis in Values." A Learning cluster consisted of the forums, "The Future of Learning: Into the Twenty-First Century," "Creativity and the Learning Process," "The Right to Lead," "Confronting Myths of Education," and "Educational Hardware: Destructive or Instructive?" A Children's Health cluster was composed of forums devoted to topics of health protection and disease prevention, delivery of health care services, and consideration of children with handicaps and injuries. A Parents and Family cluster dealt with the forum topics, "Changing Families in a Changing Society," "Children and Parents: Together in the World," "Family Planning and Family Economics," and "Developmental Day-care Services for Children," probably the most closely observed of all the forums. Everywhere one saw day-care buttons, although no conference day-care program was arranged. A few fortunate persons were moved by an imperfect and thereby even more powerful presentation of a small drama, *A Place for Henry.*

Six members of the Watts Theater Workshop had been flown across America to perform, in a crowded hotel meeting room with inadequate space and lighting, a play of simple plot in which an unseen son of decent human beings is accidentally electrocuted because he is not properly cared for by a sitter. We never see the child, Henry. We see only his mortified mother and angered father being restrained and supported by a grandmother and a neighbor couple who must help the mother resolve her pride and the father, his submissiveness, in order to prepare for the act of having more children. The actors and directors were black. Their offstage attire was entirely black. For their performance I sat in the front row. The stage, such as it was, began practically at my feet, and several times I could have reached out and touched any of the actors or handled the props. All that blackness at a White House conference. All that humanity in the souls of six simple human beings. That staying thunderbolt of life in a transitory carnival of words and deeds and promises constituting a transitory scenario of people talking, talking, talking together.

Two more clusters completed the convention's roster. Communities and Environments contained the forums, "Children Without Prejudice," "It's All Where You Live: Children, Their

Physical and Social Environments," "Child Development and
the Mass Media," and "The Child and Leisure Time." Finally,
the Laws, Rights, and Responsibilities cluster combined forums dealing with "The Rights of Children," "Children in
Trouble: Alternatives to Delinquency, Abuse, and Neglect,"
"The Child Advocate," and "About the Law: Communicating the Law's Message to Children."

How much the White House actually influenced the choice
of forum chairpersons, vice chairpersons, and memberships,
usually about sixteen per forum, is not known. Though participants continually complained about the proverbial "setup,"
a staff member reported a White House indifference and noted that on one occasion, Hess had told his own superiors they
would have to let him appoint his selections or he would quit.
("I thought the arrangements were marvelous," a woman said.
"We were preselected but we have a cross section here. In our
forum we have a black mother and a blind boy.") What did
happen is that upon the suggestion of hundreds of people and
organizations, forum topics were developed, state chairpersons selected their delegates—a status distinct from forum
member—and forum chairpersons were assigned responsibility
for preparing rather lengthy working papers from which their
forums hopefully would meet the goals of the conference,
namely to "pursue the problems of children through examination," "to establish priorities," "to predict problems," "to
provide a national forum for the exchange of ideas," "to identify, encourage and solicit participation," and "to establish
orderly and effective procedures for implementation and administration of whatever proposals and ideas would come
forth." It was in this last category, "the establishment of
orderly and effective procedures," that some misjudgment
may have been made. Irrespective for the moment of what
substantively took place—and a great deal did take place, despite the fact that participants were instructed to work with
documents on which they had not collaborated—a conference
of this nature reveals that the so-called man and woman on
the street know a great deal, feel even more, sense keenly a
desertion, or disenfranchisement if not alienation, and through
television in particular have learned about politics. They may
be coarse politics, crude and insensitive politics, they may ev-
en seem to be self-indulgent and childish, gaudy caricatures
of what the professionals slough off with minimal effort. But

it is politics, and for the conference to omit a plenary session was for the more political participants a degrading omission, an unforgivable assessment, a perfect misdiagnosis.

So from all over they came: deans and professors, students, poets, mothers, fathers, the top-dogs of organizations, the near-to-the-bottom-dogs as well, and some of them on society's firing lines (although these people, surprisingly, were quick to speak of their own peculiar passivity). Then, weighed down with schedules, lists of meeting rooms, and announcements of special events—like film showings, workshops with artists, Haim Ginott, Kenneth Koch, and an Atlanta drama group, musical events, demonstrations of all sorts, concerts and miniconcerts like the one in which a group of children entered a forum, sang a chorus of "Over There" and departed, photographic exhibitions, field trips to local schools and hospitals, videotape showings, graphics, cartoons, sensitivity training, fantasy simulation games, role playing, synectics, improvisational training, dance groups, selected bibliographies, puppet shows, staged injury situations, psycho-socio-drama—and overwhelmed by an endless parade of people with badges decorated with a little green stem and red dot bud flower which said, I suppose, children, grace, growth, and loveliness, they began to sculpt the wording for proposals and priorities.

To summarize the hundreds of pages of working reports is impossible. As I walked in and out of the rooms where forum members met, sometimes huddled around a table, sometimes as an audience listening to a senator ("We need to do for America's children what Nader did for G.M.") or film-maker, a psychologist or nurse, I began to feel as though the conference set was indeed a carnival, its wondrous booths having been constructed overnight among the streets of an unfamiliar neighborhood. The current of people, moreover, seemed to keep us from the one booth, the one special ride where magically all truth might be finalized. Always we walked with the knowledge that soon an imagined once-in-a-lifetime chance would disappear, the booths would be torn down, the people would vanish, and the ugly streets and storefronts would return.

They spoke often of personality formation in the forum meetings, the effect of parents, religion and ethics on the early years of child development, and how parents still don't know enough about the emergence of that thing called "identity" in the smaller persons who carry their genes. ("What we need is a 'Sesame Street' for adults," a man said.) They spoke of child environments, of trees and parks and land use. One group even built a miniature physical environment. I caught them there speaking of a child's world while sitting in children's chairs and dropping their cigarette ashes onto, I suppose, a child's floor. Forum members spoke of the profane and dehumanizing values of American institutions, of the crisis of values and of self-centered children in suburbs and disadvantaged children in the cities. The rhetoric, passwords, and behavioral formulae are everywhere now. Organizations, they said again and again, would have to alter their priorities, for families had to be made stable. Work, religion, leisure time activities had to be reordered so that children might taste the delights of accomplishments and productivity that with patience and protection, can emerge from their talents and specialness. ("If a person has a personality he can sell," a woman said, "and be involved, he can get anywhere. If I can, anybody can. I hope a black wants to.") Education too, would have to undergo a mighty change. Free schools, experimental schools, and whole new options for learning would have to come into existence by the twenty-first century. Maybe the nation's 200th birthday would be a propitious time "for a nationwide dialogue about our entire learning enterprise." Training programs, members reasoned, would have to be established with the nurturance of creativity as one of many prime ideals. This would mean that all sorts of resources would be mined from communities, and hence, the credentialism that probably restricts us as often as it guards us might have to be modified.

In a room where high school seniors had danced a few nights before, a group was speaking about a goal of national literacy. They agreed that government assistance was essential. Another group believed the government could help to dispel myths of education like, "children have to go to school to learn," or "there is one best way to educate," or "you can't do anything without money." Everywhere, people were discussing the process of education and the significance of individual learning rates in a culture pushing systematized technology and advancement. "Humanness is forgotten," they agreed in one ballroom, for educational hardware has become the salient concern of too many teachers and scientists. In another ballroom we were treated to an experience of just such hardware. A professor advised us to get involved, relax, and let it all roll over us, "it" being the colossal holograph which some insisted on calling the holocaust. Consisting of an enormous viewing screen, some sixteen slide projectors, several movie projectors, a complex machine for mixing these media inputs, a laser beam producing three-dimensional images in space, and two trained, headphoned professionals to coordinate the whole thing, some nine simultaneous visual images and a few audio stimuli rolled over us, yielding a learning effect that might some day make group dynamics in the classroom look as foolishly antiquated as a buck lateral series off the single wing. And I, in my day, had thought colored chalk to be such a lovely innovation.

In another room we found ourselves communicating nonverbally with lovely damsels or high school administrators or picking fights with strangers in order to prepare ourselves for a sensitivity training drama about high school political rebellion. In another room Jane Elliot had made a bunch of people screaming mad, as her exercise in the experiencing of prejudice, in which brown-eyed people "confront" blue-eyed people, had taken most but not all of them by storm. A fair young lady with golden hair looked deep into my eyes as I innocently entered the room. I loved it. A chunk of Eros in the middle of the midway. For the moment I though she would offer something in the vein of the college freshman who, taking pity on the rings under my eyes and the tremor in my note-taking hand, had offered to split the one joint she had brought to the convention. But the young woman was hunting for pigment, not action, and suddenly I heard her voice for the first time, soft and mellow as the old Danny Kaye record went: "Get out, you brown-eyed bastard!" Traumatized I caught the lovely face of a man near by with handsome blue eyes reading the *New York Times.* His flowered badge read "Diaz, New York." He gave me a look and said, "Don't ask me. I just got off the boat."

In the forums on health and handicapped children there were no such exercises. Early diagnosis and proper treatment, and generally the delivery of care to children were on everyone's minds. In forum 13, the working paper had stressed ways to avoid sociological and psychological as well as physical accidents to children. The mood of the health reports and their actual forum meetings were usually deadly serious. Other reports noted the problems of family roles, the pressure

particularly on women, and the nature of delinquency, alienation, and violence. In the report of forum 15 someone wrote:
"Needed is a change in our patterns of living to once again
bring people back into the lives of children and children back
into the lives of people." Children, another report urged,
should have more responsibility. They should be included in
the world of adults and by having full voting rights on all
committees—including school boards which make decisions
about children—they should earn the true power they require
in society. ("Put 'em where we'll trip over 'em," a woman said.)
Then again, family planning and population policies generally
would have to be implemented. Families would have to be assured a certain minimal income and be provided with adequate
day-care centers which conceivably occupy children for over
8,000 hours during their lifetimes. These centers would require specially trained personnel, and essentially a new definition of women's rights and women's roles. ("When women
are frustrated," a man said, "society is frustrated.") But they
would also require an end to prejudice, to subtle child neglect
and unforgivable punishment, like feeding drugs to children
because they are too hard to control, or administering psychological tests in order to scientifically differentiate populations and send them into the world in different directions:
some to the top of society, others to the bottom.

In forum 19 the report spoke of better housing conditions,
which implies restructuring community zoning laws, encouraging heterogeneous neighborhoods, and using land in more
beneficent fashion. In forum 21 creative uses of leisure time
were debated and the inherent evil of leisure, a myth left over
from a puritanical culture, was riddled with a salvo of criticism
and words like intellectual, aesthetic and spiritual growth. Finally, the rights of children, the right to know rights and laws,
good or bad, the protection and rehabilitation of those who
go the "wrong way," and the pursuit of a child advocacy
program screamed in the working papers of the high number
forums. Compassion, empathy, neglect were words used in
connection with delinquents, drop-outs, druggies and the other children who manage to fall away from those of us in the
middle.

But something was amiss. A booth had been emptied or
never erected at all. They were fighting something out in the
conference rooms; they made demands of their chairpersons;
they griped over their forum assignments; they swore behind

Mr. Hess's back; they expressed embarrassment for their being in Washington and about the money being spent on the two conferences—some three and a half million dollars—and they saw their morale topple like a depressed Dow Jones average as they asked themselves what good could possibly come of it all. Children, their rights and needs, their beauty and safety, their splendid potential and hope, were becoming nothing more than weightless symbols to use in homilies, like "mother" and "apple pie." No sir, they would leave a mark on Washington; they'd let their president know they were not about to be run through another high pressure/low action convention.

A good number of participants accordingly proposed a non-tax deductible Children's Lobby aimed at securing "enactment of needed legislation," promoting "adequate appropriations of public funds," helping "parents and other concerned adults to be effective in bringing about changes," involving "business and industry and other institutions," and encouraging "imaginative and effective administration of approved programs." Other groups similarly proposed an Institute for Child Development and the Mass Media (forum 20); a Commission for the Next Generation (forum 19); special committees on racism and peace (forum 24); a high status child advocate possibly to be made a function of the vice-president's office; a presidential committee to protect the rights of families that fall outside the "two-parent" form (forum 14); a commission for children and families charged with altering personnel policies and ending child exploitation in any form of commercialism (forum 15); and a presidential task force establishing a fund for children's services as well as for broadening the understanding of day-care needs (forum 17). This same forum had also come out publicly against Senator Long's Federal Child Care Corporation Act, on the grounds that the bill set inadequate financial standards and necessarily would fund undesirable custodial programs. All the while, other groups, strangers the day before but now political brothers and sisters not yet recognizing their own magnitude and membership, struggled to produce what ultimately emerged as a double-header plenary session.

On Wednesday, two nights before the conference would end, a so-called minority caucus that had allied blacks, browns, Spanish-speaking/Spanish-surname people along with women's liberation members, presented what they called a plenary

session. There were speeches and recitations by local minis-
ters, author Piri Thomas, a young Panther, and a native American from the Midwest who, after remarking that he learned
not American history in school but the history of an immigrant people, asked humbly that America give back what already belonged to the native Americans. In the end, however,
the presence of Hosea Williams and the evening's final address
by Rev. Ralph Abernathy—in which races and classes were
miraculously conjoined somehow—made the event especially
legitimate and especially prominent. At that meeting some
sixty-seven demands were passed as chairperson Charles Hurst,
pride beaming in his eyes and a twinkle of victory heard in
his voice, asked those supporting the demands to say "Aye,"
and those opposing them to stand up. Applause greeted his
words that the proposals would be taken directly to the White
House. But how could anyone oppose positions to end racism
and oppression, give equal opportunity to all people and adequate financial support ($6,500 per year) to all families, guar-
antee that children everywhere receive proper medical care
and educational facilities, and be protected and not victimized by laws? For those who care about such things, the minority caucus withdrew an earlier recommendation to relieve
Mr. Hess of his duties and substitute Dr. Hurst, the president
of Chicago's Malcolm X College. The caucus boycotted no
conference activity, but in turning their badges upside down,
they expressed gross dissatisfaction with the entire structure
of the week and their intolerance of the upside-downness of
the convention's priorities. Upon unanimous acceptance of
the caucus's proposals, badges were again flipped right side
up, and so the little green and red flowers, which reversed
had become dainty Christmas bushes, were now righted. An
integrity, a union of people was born that night; sentimental
perhaps, but lovely and hopeful. ("We're together now," someone said. "God, look at us. We're together now!")

On the following evening a second self-designated plenary
session was held, presumably sponsored by the Council for
National Organizations on Children. The mood now was anxious, almost frantic. The acclaimed resolutions which took
well over five hours to produce ranged from a guaranteed an-
nual income to opposition to the SST project, war, racism,
pollution, poverty, and hunger, to a demand that the president sign the bill funding Head Start programs, to a request
for a systematic study of genetic propensities, to a demand

that television advertise only the truth, to support for day care. The morale, which had dipped, was now shedding anger and certainly little was helped by the president's veto on that very Wednesday of the Comprehensive Manpower Bill. Not ironically, forum 16 had issued a document the previous day stating that "the first priority in the area of family economics is to expand the job market to provide for employment of all those who seek a job. . . . Manpower training and incentive programs will play a key role in preparing individuals to find their best possible places within either the public or the private sector." Thus, if anyone felt this last-ditch brand of politics to be overly self-indulgent or wasteful, then let them tell what had been achieved lo these many years by voting the straight and silent way. The makeshift plenary sessions would be the closest some would ever come to the machinery, to the people, to the Man, and to the city of politics. If Senator Bayh wanted to speak at this one session, if that's what his presence at one o'clock in the morning meant, then he would have to wait his turn because the lines of delegates waiting for air time at each floor microphone would give way to no one.

By Friday afternoon, most of the delegates had left Washington. The hotel lobbies and meeting rooms heaved exhaustion, and papers were strewn everywhere, left on floors and furniture for a preponderantly black hotel staff to clean up. Those that remained in the morning watched a movie made by the conference's organization. In response to organizing an official plenary session, Mr. Hess, supported by several forum chairpersons, had countered with a plan calling for forum and cluster chairpersons to draw up lists of their groups' overriding concerns and specific forum recommendations. In addition, any caucus procuring two hundred signatures could put forward one such concern. In the movie, the entire convention would hear various chairpersons read back-up statements to these recommendations and then everyone would vote, first by ranking their priority of the sixteen concerns and next by checking off six of twenty-four recommendations. The rationale for such a procedure, according to Mr. Hess, was that a typical plenary session would have given an average of about one minute of air time to each conferee and preclude an opportunity for a dialogue (that overworked word).

The media, the mood, the mania, the proportions of it all, Washington, had won out. ("Not everything has to be at a national level," someone comforted us. "We can't all be po-

litical, you know.'') At ten o'clock Friday evening, ten hours
after the official closing time of the conference, members of
the press, television, and radio hounded a tired lot of loyal
souls counting, checking, verifying ballots on which some
four thousand Americans had expressed their choice of overriding concerns. It all seemed utterly pathetic to some that
with so much to be done, it, the conference, America, had
come down to this: a parent admonishing a child: apple pie,
jello, or ice cream, but not all three. The evening moved on
and we waited, all of us like TV anchormen joking about
some barometric voting community, and begging for some
hint of the winning priorities and through them, how a rearranged America might look tomorrow.

One could not come away from this event, from this ordeal with a single thought, with one lead-in or headline. If
only we could write like that holograph so that nine, twelve,
a billion messages could be transmitted at once, and so that
simultaneously all the visual and audio stimuli of those six
December days could reach everyone. Then all could hear the
many times television and textbooks were rapped for perpe-
trating disease and prejudice, and for desecrating children's
imaginations. (Television, a psychiatrist lamented, was just
like all the experts: teaching us how to feel, how to think,
and how to decide.) Then too, the raucus good humor in the
Olympia Bar and hotel coffee shops could be heard at the
same time that a man proposed dedicating the conference's
final report to those children who never benefited from the
1960 White House Conference but who died in Vietnam all
the same; at the same time organization leaders, sponsors,
academicians, and practitioners spoke of their private enterprises and interests and hidden agendas; at the same time a
Spanish-surname gentleman, in urging the legalization of
Spanish, recited the statistic that thirty thousand California
school children were diagnosed retarded because no one took
account of the fact that they didn't speak English; at the
same time a young Chicano told of the hundreds of children
who died because language barriers prevented people from
reaching telephone operators, doctors, or police, and from
signing adequate hospital health forms; at the same time two
young Chicanos sought out press members to express their
fear that the minority caucus demands had gypped them; at
the same time that a Minnesota Indian described finding his
daughter weeping before the television set, rooting for the

cowboys because she simply could not stand being a loser any longer; at the same time that other parents found themselves coming disassembled, detached, not from children exactly, but from their own childhoods. And through it all, the constant image of human beings forgotten, mismanaged, homeless, splintered, dehumanized.

Does this all make one a bleeding heart? An archetype of Charles Reich's consciousness II? The sounds, actions and purposes, the visions, like the presence of "so many" black people (although less than eight percent of the conference was in fact black), and the races walking, talking, partying, sexing together, whites deferring to blacks in crowded lobbies, actually moving their bodies to make space for them, made so much sense even though at the time bunches of weary people agreed that the conference was by definition foolish, useless and out of control. ("As a boy, we used to debate so long on what we would do with the money we would make collecting bottles," someone said, "that we never ever collected any bottles.") Weeks later someone asked whether there had been "real kids" there. A youth caucus did meet but according to one person was "disrupted" by certain "types." The press did not attend their caucus but youth would have their qualified day, many days in fact, under the glorious blue skies of Colorado where adults, free of responsibilities and telephones, could give them full attention, and where no college campus could impose its styles of rhetoric, politics, and ideologies.

But in the meantime, did whoever listens to these things in Washington hear us? Did they see us? And, as Piri Thomas asked several times on that Wednesday night of the minority caucus plenary session, "Did they dig it?"

The journal closed on her lap. Erlene Menter lay back in her chair, her legs stretched out, her eyes wide open, looking high into the corner of the small room as if there might be something up there for her to read. "They sure do write hard English," she finally said. "By the time you get around to reading the thing, then understanding it, it sure seems as though you've been on a long, long, long trip. Now you tell me, do you really think any scientist or what you call doctor, is going to understand what my life is really like? Are you going to tell me that these fellows with all their books and schooling are going to have the slightest eyeful of this room, and the kids? Why, if they saw this mess they'd up and leave in a minute, and you know they would. The students, well, they're different. They come around here with their jabbering and all, all excited, ready to make trouble; they're gonna make war on the world if anybody'd give them half a chance. They're like you. They got these little pieces of paper for me to read about housing, and busing, and welfare laws. Some of it makes good sense, like they know those rules about welfare. Don't you kid yourself for a minute. They know those rules and most of them aren't even lawyers."

To read the essays, documented as they were with the figures of certainty and authenticity, was to be invaded, molested, swallowed up by the rough-grained pictures of professionals who, in a funny way, had no business being there at all. It was not the explicit political position of these articles that hurt, as much as the sense that sacred proprieties had been ignored. It was as though curfew laws had been violated by the very men who had established them in the first place.

Evidently, Kathleen Cavanaugh had been waiting eagerly for my arrival. Though I was on time, she acted as if I'd kept her waiting three hours for our appointment. She was steaming mad, more upset than I'd ever seen her, even more so than the time we had spoken of Robert Kennedy's death. Her self-proclaimed period of mourning concluded, a time of uncontrollable anger had overtaken her. She just didn't know what to do with all that anger, and my suggestion that we take a walk didn't seem to help.

But on this more recent occasion, the seventy-three-year-old widow was burning. She was all but ready to pounce on me when I knocked. Usually I would see her through the glass, descending the long staircase, straightening her skirt

just as she would reach the inside of the door. This day, however, she was peering out, surveying the street as if forewarned
of an impending accident.

"I've read it. That pack of lies. Who in the name of you-
know-who gave you something like that to give to me? Why
the nerve of those people. Say, Thomas, they're not friends
of yours, are they? That's good. Think of that. Here I am
shooting my mouth off and maybe saying things about your
friends. But they couldn't be. That's good. A man's got to be
real careful saying those things. Why there's not a morsel of
truth in that. I've been alive on this good earth almost seven-
ty-four years. Even a woman doesn't go to high school learns
something in that time. You have to, raising your children
and all. I showed this to the boys upstairs. You know I told
you I rent the upstairs to those students. Well, they agreed
with me. One said he'd read something the other day which
says just the opposite. Now how's that possible? Either these
are real facts or they're make-believe, and scientists don't
make things up, at least the ones on TV I see don't make
things up." We laughed at that.

Two women, anyway, were unable to discover in these
pages the truly valued aspects of their lives. Supposedly they
were to see themselves on the neatly printed page, but all
that emerged were tragic distortions of themselves and of
their worlds. Somewhere the essence of their lives had been
lost in the waves of categories, data analyses, and discussions
of findings. Suddenly there had emerged on the clean, white
paper mere content, samples, not of people whom they did
not know nor barely recognized, but of themselves.

The trip to Hannah Brachman's was always interesting.
Traveling down Blue Hill Avenue revealed a panorama of Boston's social history. How many students had come to this area
to make their own studies, and then described their impressions of the soul food stores alongside the kosher butcher
shops, or the Mogen Davids adorning the fronts of record
and barber shops. Most everyone around Boston knows the
"story" of blacks moving in, Jews moving out, and the exo-
dus of the young and affluent to Brookline and Newton.

Mrs. Brachman was always waiting for me, some food prepared, a neighbor's child reading in the kitchen, eager to make
friends with someone from the university. Our discussions usu-

ally centered on her feelings about her family, Jewish writers and scholars, events in New York, Jerusalem, and at Brandeis. Always she would have words of praise for the president of Brandeis but harsher words for blacks occupying buildings and demanding that a university's name be changed. Mrs. Brachman's loyalties were coming out more strongly. "Who helped us?" she would ask rhetorically. "Who marched down Fifth Avenue or sat in buildings or made revolution for *us*? They still don't do anything for us."

As a favor, Mrs. Brachman read a couple of articles written by social scientists on the activities of Jews in the New Left and the rather significant position of power they seemed to have attained. We both agreed that the pieces were written from sympathetic viewpoints, the authors presumably remaining as objective as possible. The data, I had thought, were well-collected, thoughtfully analyzed, and presented without bias. "You can't argue with those numbers. It's hard to fight that. It seems pretty obvious." Soon her eyes moved away from the pages of the reprints, now wrinkled and torn. "You know, not a lot of people know it, but the Jews have done a lot for this country. When you stop to think of all the doctors and lawyers, all the professors, it's really something. It's really some accomplishment. Look at Israel. Is that not something extraordinary? The fears, the wars. What these people have suffered. From one war right into that trouble. What's going to happen? What's going to happen?"

Where in this is the reality our students want us to discover as they yank us into the world hoping that our observations might be more accurate, our recommendations for change more influential? How are we able to differentiate our research intentions from our policy-making intentions? And how can we separate our desire to make science from a publisher's or reader's desire to make politics?

"What about the article, Mrs. Menter?"

"Oh yes. Well I don't care what he says here. I know about that report and this report and that report. You don't need to tell Negroes about that stuff. That's white man's words for white man's ears. When the Negro professors start writing things, you'll see a whole different picture. You go out and bring me some of *their* work and you'll get a different picture. You'll get a very different picture."

Erlene Menter knew full well the contents of the eight-page article I had asked her to read. When all the grammar, paragraphs, and data had been pushed aside, she saw a terrifying message. She had read eight pages about black children growing up in ghettos, about absent fathers, the occurrence of incest and the impact of all this on children and on a group of people who were struggling to find a pattern that might simultaneously knit them together and lift them all up to a level where they wouldn't receive such devastating rebukes or, for that matter, such perplexing triumphs. The message she received was that when this scientist ran his figures and numbers through a computing machine, it came out, as she said, "that the Negroes aren't getting anywhere in particular, too fast."

Debates on the possibility of "value-free" social science are becoming increasingly rare. Some social scientists believe that they can make so-called value-free contributions to fact and theory. Others are sure that such freedom from bias can never be achieved, if due only to the more subtle implications of the very act of publishing from a position within a university.

As effortful as each day has become in the eighteen years since her mother died of a heart attack in the house where Kathleen still lives, Kathleen Cavanaugh fulfilled her promise to me by reading twenty rather trying pages on the value and belief systems of "working-class" Catholic families. I picked the piece mainly because we had spoken of such matters before, and because it seemed to me that the authors had captured without distortion the lives of people "sociologically similar" to Mrs. Cavanaugh. I had thought she would immediately read of a familiar world, accurately presented. Diligently and methodically she had read the assignment, even taking notes on the inside of the telephone book in that delicate thin-line handwriting of hers.

"Are they teaching this kind of stuff at school? Because if they are, you could sure do a good thing for these students by telling each and every single one just what we do believe. Don't you let them get away with this. I'll bet you those professors never did speak with any of those people they write about. No one talks like that, unless he's composing something, like a story or poem."

Kathleen Cavanaugh was profoundly upset. The article had

portrayed something insidious, and she felt betrayed. It was
as though her pride had been extinguished, her soul invaded
and found dry and hollow. She had learned more, she would
say later on, from television, even though it too "favors what
the rich people have to say and think. And buy." By what
had seemed to me to be an insightful, penetrating glance at a
community's social life, Mrs. Cavanaugh had been shot down,
right in her steps.

It seems almost impossible to publish a report that represents no political bias or implies no political action. Whatever
our intention, whatever our assumptions of how value-free
our research can be, the implications stay with us. Even with
our modest intentions to "advance science or knowledge,"
the popular media and its readers stand ready to greet the applications or the political implications. What, they ask, are
the products or profits and the statements of appropriate action to be found in these writings? What can I take and use of
this? How can it be reduced to the solid, true laws of human
nature that, after all, these scholars are supposed to be dis-
covering?

To these questions, social scientists respond with troubled
ambivalence. Many people have pressured academicians to derive with certainty the state of human nature and programs
for upgrading everyone. Working against this, naturally, are
the "limitations of the art" as well as, perhaps, a primordial
reluctance to explain mankind, to explain so much variance
that futures become predictable, presents explicable, pasts
logical, and certainties guaranteed. There may be a primitive
sense in each of us that will forever prevent a total explana-
tion or perfect experiment. Yet if such a sense exists, it may
not be tolerated by audiences demanding exactitude in diagnosis and treatment.

Still, we do little to convey to these audiences the tentativeness and possible inaccuracy of our statements. There are
those of us who qualify their televised pronouncements with
"we know very little" or "our science is so young," only to
proceed to deadly pontification. Others advance the most
recently achieved knowledge while ignoring the attendant
responsibility of their published words.

Recently, a young social psychologist bemoaned the overnight success of his first book. He had received letters from
countless people asking him whether they could take his tests

and undergo his experiments, which somehow were supposed
to better their lives. What shocked the author, really, was the
way people "could just take over my book and do with it
whatever they wanted." He was no longer in control. From
even a cursory reading his readers had come away with political and social strands he himself barely recognized. Where he
had used data to reinforce hunches, they had clutched that
data as proof of the book's "real" message. They had skipped
over the pages where conceptualizations were embellished
and had rushed to the meaty parts from which they might
take something for themselves. Now they begged him to let
them be a part of his grand scheme for change and success.
There seemed to be nothing in their reactions suggesting an
appreciation for any intellectual contribution. "They read
that book as though it were a manual on how to ice skate!"

His book was taken as a manual because in part, the media
of popular communication cannot always tolerate messages
of what intellectuals think about, work with, indeed, play
with. Popular media cannot always permit the luxury of theoretical reasoning or development, nor can they spend time
dealing with contributions to the history of theory when there
are hard, cold facts to be gotten out and publicized. Moreover,
there must be a splash, a glimmer, a scintillating explosion
in every published pronouncement or it won't "catch on."
There must be something that one can hold in one's hand, a
"fistful of reality," as Sartre said.

The conflicting needs of scientists as against those of their
publishers, readers and, increasingly, students, make it pro-
gressively more difficult to "get away with" pure and simple
contributions to theory and methodology. Despite the many
failures and the flood of contradictory books and reports,
much of the public remains loyal to the belief that social scientists are experts, suppliers of the right sort of knowledge.
In a word, their expertise renders them "solutionists." Their
ideas cannot stay as ideas, but must be translated into facts
and answers. As speedily as these ideas pass from the page to
the eye, they lose their tentativeness and "hunchiness" and
become certainty if not plans for action.

Erlene Menter was laughing again, sitting up straight and
pushing the journal back across the table. As it moved, she
rotated it slightly, the letters now right-side-up for her. "Nice

colors they use," she said, staring at the cover and fondling
its smoothness, as though the outline of each letter might
stand up high enough so that she could touch it, then read it
with her eyes closed. She let the pages riffle gently along the
tips of her fingers, then a few times more. "The paper's nice
too. Not like the newspaper."

The article had said as much through its authoritative and
bookish appearance as it had through the statements on its
pages.

Just as what we study represents a real system of values, so
too do the "products" of our studies perpetuate these values
and hold them up as some ideal, however temporary. A popular conception holds that in science, publication implies certainty. Clearly, too much certainty is taken for granted.
Among most readers, even editors, scientists simply do not
play with ideas. Tentativeness and unsureness cannot be accepted from them. Maybe that's why correlations too often
emerge as causation, and why summaries of findings become
publicized as incontestable facts.

For Hannah Brachman, a mythic tradition of intellectualism and achievement, spirit and honor along with suffering,
welled up within the soul she wished to share with millions of
people. The two studies she had read were bad press; but they
could not be denied or forgotten. Scientists teach facts, and
the facts they had taught her were that Jewish boys and girls
were being disruptive, causing problems, getting themselves
into trouble, and going to jail. For her, science is facts, undeniable, incontrovertible facts. "When a man with such education, such erudition speaks, he knows what he's talking about.
Maybe I'd like to disagree. To tell you the truth I wish he
hadn't written this. Or maybe I wish you hadn't brought it to
me. But that's the world. That's the world. It seems a shame."

Some people, naturally, have adopted the findings of the
social sciences and found them valuable for their work and
for their lives. But the day is not yet here when the public
fully appreciates the playfulness of ideas or the fun and excitement of knowledge. Not enough people yet understand
the little boy or girl, free from everything and everyone, alone
in a room, engrossed in a task only angels dare understand.

Surely there still exists the popular conception of profes-

sors as people who are "only playing." This is the notion that
speaks to their lack of any tangible product or of "an honest
day's work" and concludes that professors remain as childish-
ly occupied as the children they teach.

This is hardly the same view as that held by academics
about the playfulness of ideas inside the academy. The evolution of intellectualism, just as the development of cognitive
abilities in the child, brings cultures to the point where ideas
almost stand by themselves, seemingly unencumbered by a
political association with some greater shared reality. Indeed,
the highest form of thought permits both the capacity to imagine the impossible or unreal and the capacity to play with
ideas, to work with and sculpt them, even if the final product
fails to yield anything but joy.

As students argue louder than ever before, only the elite
can still afford the luxury of such playfulness and tentativeness. Only the elite can dare consider "intellectual contributions" sufficient. Yet they must be made. Many students
have joined the public in crying for political products and not
playfulness. So faculty members now fear the end of purely
"academic days" as they struggle to defend themselves against
what they feel to be an onslaught of anti-intellectualism, anti-
rationalism, anti-objectivism, and anti-science led by, of all
people, their very disciples and apprentices.

"Think of the money spent trying to figure out what's happening in these neighborhoods. That other book you had
JoAnne [her daughter] read was all about black folks in Baltimore and Washington. Think of that. They go all the way
to Baltimore just to look into their homes when they could
come right here. They're all welcome right here. You tell
them if they want to make some of their studies, they should
come and see me. I'll tell them stories they can write ten
books about, fifty books about if their hands don't get tired
and those machines of theirs don't die."

"I think maybe those studies were done by people who
lived in Baltimore and Washington."

"Maybe so. I thought JoAnne said something about going
all the way down there to make their studies. You don't hear
anything about this neighborhood, 'cepting that there's trouble with the welfare boards and those . . . Man, they've got a

collection of people working for them, you wouldn't believe your eyes."

Two sorts of familiar political spectrums have emerged: the "horizontal" scale to the left and right of moderate, and the "vertical" scale about which students are reminding us. The vertical scale extends from elite privilege to disenfranchisement. Coming from a generation of objectivity, some students have long advocated total awareness of this spectrum but now demand direct participation in the lives of disenfranchised and oppressed people.

The university model of detachment and noninvolvement was seriously shaken by the Civil Rights movement of the 1960s. The initial student involvement in the lives of southern blacks led to student emphasis on political intervention and on becoming implicated. Sit-ins turned to voter registration and redistricting campaigns. But the intellectuals remained a step behind, some reporting on the events in the North and South, many banging out research documents investigating the parents, grandparents, school problems, and generalized psychopathologies of student workers. Nevertheless, the result for many scholars was a violent shift from playfulness and sovereign academic goals to a politicization of their research in a way that would, as they say, help mankind. At the very least, this new breed of social scientist was thinking about the concrete products of their enterprises and the implications these products might have in the political arena. For them academia was a necessary home, and tentativeness a necessary constraint, not a way of increasing the distance between themselves and a population for whom they cared, and at times, for whom they grieved. They wanted and needed to be in touch.

JoAnne Menter sat cross-legged on the floor; two friends slouched on the sofa listening to her read sections from a book. As she recited certain passages she had carefully marked earlier, her friends screamed with laughter, bouncing up and down on the floor and furniture. JoAnne would start another passage, and they would cackle and jabber. "You better believe it, baby. This cat sets up right there on the corner . . ." And they would roar. I couldn't help laughing myself. Erlene, working about the room as though she weren't paying the four of us any attention, showed by an occasional glance that she would just as soon send all of us maniacs to some institution. But she too understood.

As civil rights movements and Vietnam aroused many students from the pleasantries of psychological reasoning into the more profane realms of sociology and political or policy sciences, an implicit hope developed that social science would not only be "relevant," but chock full of policy implications. Some scientists responded directly by sitting on government commissions; others responded less directly by consulting, a tenuous process in which, almost rheostatically, they could control the amount of their commitment and involvement. Despite a prevalent anti-intellectualism, the contention persists—an almost spiritual contention—that knowledge is power and with it no limits need be set. Surely if we can get to the moon, we can get to cities, suburbs, Appalachia, southern Texas and Florida. Nonetheless, while some scientists dive headlong into the explicit politics of their research, others seek to wiggle out of the politics of certainty. Not wishing to participate in intellectualized politics of confrontation, they strive to keep their distance, if not necessarily their "disinterestedness." They too, however, have become aware of the political implications of their work and, perhaps, are becoming aware of their place in that vertical spectrum, and the ways in which they support it.

Political self-consciousness has grown to the point where we recognize and confess to the more obvious implications of our printed statements and of our acts of publishing. No one needs to be told, for example, that in such areas as "race relations" debates in the literature or disagreements over interpretations of data or over the assessment of methodological procedures have more than a latent political impact. This we know. But are we always able or willing to react to research pronouncements that do not seem to us to be so "touchy"—for example, studies of working-class Catholics or the activities of Jews in the New Left? Do we shudder, in fact, from the politics embedded in gigantic volumes of theoretical scripture? Are we not reading theoretical expositions in part for the politics they might bequeath? Are we, because of the people who read us and publish us, becoming aware of touchiness and relevance, discreteness and ethicality, against a back-

drop which heretofore has been infrequently used? And,
from all of these issues, may we ever again claim objectivity,
or freedom from politics and elitism?

"Did the articles remind you of anything, Mrs. Brachman?"
"The articles. Two professors are telling me that this college business is being run by Jews. Jewish boys and Jewish
girls. This part I can't figure out at all. What business is it of
the girls? If they're going to get into trouble, at least it should
be the boys. What do these girls know? They're so young.
They're so small. Aren't they interested in . . . in . . . in growing up, with homes, with husbands, with children! What's it
coming to with Negroes fighting with the police, with boys
and girls in the schools fighting with their teachers? They
should go without a little bit, they'd see how you fight with
policemen!"

Some scholars now notice the more subtle political strains
which silently contribute to the kinds of research topics chos-
en by scientists and the sort of research acceptable to publishers and the reading public. While scientists need not think in
these terms, no one can doubt the fads and ritualized sources
of inquiry generated and perpetuated in the social sciences. In
fact, they have been studied. But fads themselves are steeped
in politics. Thus, journals and magazines propagate politics
when they select topics or writers whose extravagant or subtle polemics go in the "proper" direction. One finds, for
example, mountains of articles on city schools but nary a
molehill on the problems in suburban high schools, apart
from drugs, long hair, and dress codes. There is more than
one can read on working-class patterns but surprisingly little
on the upper middle class.

Kathleen Cavanaugh pounded her fist on the open pages:
"They're just not going to pin me down that easily." JoAnne
Menter, too, had rebuked the characterization of "her people." Her laughter hardly masked the poignancy of the book
and her desperate attempts to free herself from the shackles
of categories, divisions of populations, and conceptualizations made by some "smart guy who thinks he knows us just
'cause he's been to school longer than us." As much as they
fought to stay abreast of groups, collectives, cultures, and
hordes of people they could hardly imagine—even after at-

tending a giant rally for black people—Erlene Menter and her daughter fought hardest of all to maintain their own beings, their own singular identities. "Before anything else," JoAnne would say, "I am always me. Somebody told me that God exists in each of us and that we should be proud just to be ourselves. So, I'm going to be me, and if people don't like it. . . ."

Politicized students have managed to convince many academics that even if they shy away from research that has explicit policy implications or from polemical pieces which unequivocally indicate their political persuasion, the very actions of research and writing can be deemed "elitist." Our concern as academics for the working class or the blacks or the young is lovely to behold, they argue, but when we offer our ideas, weighted as they are by our proclaimed status, these ideas cannot help but be blighted by the dispositions of our enterprises and by the politics of our lives and life styles. Like air bubbles, politics has been pumped into the research of people who believed they had worked diligently to make certain none would be found.

The day may never come when students succeed in pushing scholars into what they perceive as reality. By this they mean not only that intellectuals should become involved, engaged, politicized, but that they should be aware of the political electricity that illuminates their writing, and acts to legitimate their cause and freedom. Many students cannot condone the political elitism of studies and offerings which, in their very prose, protect and increase the distance between us and those we study. How often, they ask, do we consider the pretense at objectivity which removes us from the world in which we observe and write and think? How often, they ask, do we take seriously the political positions from which our writings unwittingly take shape and from which policy statements ultimately are drawn? Always they throw that word elitism at us in an effort to extinguish our habits of playfulness and immodest indifference. They want us out of our offices and into the world. Many of them want our voices to come together in what they call a new politics.

One of many justifiable statements heard that rejects assuming political stances or doing explicitly policy-oriented research is that these actions too easily lead to governmental or societal restraints on research topics and operations. There is much to fear if research is taken over by any interest group.

A paradoxical result of current student focus on the politics of professors is that one utterance can forever—publicly and inaccurately—nail a faculty member to one political position just as he or she dares to step out of his or her office and into the realities of a divided society or into what we call the field. We have yet to realize fully that the profound political implications of our work do not lie only on the left-right political spectrum in which our audience might stereotype us, but in our witting or unwitting participation in that other spectrum which contains poverty, racism, disenfranchisement, and oppression.

The most telling sign of this may be that Mrs. Cavanaugh and Mrs. Menter cannot find themselves in the articles they read. They cannot move the picture around so that it includes them. At least this is what they say. For it also may be true that the studies have found them too accurately, too penetratingly; and as sensitive human beings, they must recoil from the unintended stabs and stereotyping of these portraits.

Their reactions, therefore, might be what some would call denial. But if it is denial, it may have something to do with the fact that the studies' portraits bring them nothing more than reading materials from a friend. Their reactions may well be natural protection against a hope that more might come, that something might happen. For while we, in our debates over interpretations of data, may take time out for reanalysis, reevaluation, or even for play, they dare not leave the apartments where their children will be raised, nor the homes where their husbands died, for even a moment of fresh air.

The self-insulated separation, the lack of sensitivity to the vast and subtle political implications of our publications, in part come down to our not hearing the quiet phrases and the ritualized language forms which too often go unnoticed. When I left Mrs. Brachman for the last time, she walked me to the door of the apartment, always so neat and open to guests and family. Then she looked me squarely in the eyes, without shame and without defiance: "When you're done with your work and you have a little time on your hands, you'll go with your wife and you'll get a haircut, and then maybe you'll find some time to come back and we'll talk a little. The three of us. O.K.?"

Library of Congress Cataloging in Publication Data

Cottle, Thomas J.
Private lives and public accounts.

1. Interviewing in Sociology. 2. Participant
observation. 3. Privacy, Right of. I. Title.
HM24.C677   301'.07'23   77-73476
ISBN 0-87023-240-1